The Simple Mental Secrets of Golf

How To Make Them
Work For You

by Stan Luker
foreword by Al Geiberger

Chubasco Press

Library of Congress Card Catalogue Number 96-85471
ISBN 0-9653253-0-x

Design and Typesetting by
Words & Pictures Press
18002 Irvine Blvd., Suite 200
Tustin, CA 92780

Published by
Chubasco Press
P. O. Box 21B
Balboa Island, CA 92662-0621

Contents

Acknowledgments

Thanks to Tim Tynan, Steve Shay, Bill Burton and Mal Arenburg, good friends and golfing buddies, who helped me get my thoughts together and encouraged me to get on with it. Their willingness to review and critique early drafts helped me to keep it simple. Others who generously reviewed, edited and helped make it happen are Val Maxie, Barbara Albrecht and John Geiberger. Thanks also to PGA Professionals Mike Rheel and Sean Caligiuri who helped me to usefully describe some of the feelings of gripping the club, setting up and making a decent swing. A special thank you to Micki MacDonald, LPGA Master Professional, who, with her characteristic straightforward honesty, got me refocused on the book's objective. Special recognition is also due Alan and Maggy Graham at Words & Pictures Press for designing the layout and making it into a real book. And finally thanks to my wife, Glenda, whose encouragement and faith in me made it all worthwhile.

Foreword

A golf swing that consistently has the right tempo and flows smoothly produces the best shots. To keep your swing operating with good tempo and rhythm, your mind must keep your body under control. To play your best golf you must learn to use the power of your mind for every golf shot; but remember to keep it simple.

In my more than thirty years as a touring professional I have seen many different golf swings among my competitors and the many amateurs I have played with. I've seen players with great swings that have a terrible time playing to their potential. I have seen swings that are clearly homemade, but hit the ball beautifully and consistently. Some players seem to always be able to get the most out of their abilities, while others struggle constantly. It seems clear to me that golfers who consistently perform the best are those that have learned how to use their mind the most effectively

The most consistent golfers are those that can keep their mind and body relaxed during the whole round. In my experience a player with a relaxed mind and body is much better able to perform a competent golf swing and putting stroke.

Tension on the golf course is generally caused by an overactive mind that thinks about negative rather than positive things. Players spend far too much time analyzing and tinkering with their mechanics while they all but ignore the key role that their mind contributes to their golf swing or putting stroke.

If you can keep your mind free of negative thoughts as you play your scores will go down and more important your enjoyment will go up.

al Geiberger
"Mr. 59"

Preface

My dad played golf for enjoyment and a break from his job at the Post Office. One day he took me with him to our local muni course, a wonderful little nine hole layout. At about ten years old I didn't know anything about the game, but it was clear dad seemed to have fun. Before long he asked me if I would like to take a crack at it.

Dad gave me my first golf lesson. It was basically: "just hit it, then go find it and hit it again." He didn't take a lot of time showing me many mechanical techniques other than holding onto the club and getting set up. He showed me how to swing the club rhythmically and keep myself balanced.

My first club was out of an old golf bag we had in the garage: a dimple-faced 5 iron. For a while I followed him around the course swinging that old club at a scuffed up ball until one day he asked me if I would like to play nine holes with him. My first set of clubs consisted of my 5 iron and 3, 7, and 9 irons, a brassie, and an old blade putter. I was in heaven!

After dad's "just hit it lessons" I kept at it off and on until I could do just that. Sometimes I would hit the most wonderful shots and sometimes they were not so great. It was always fun! Whenever I played, my thinking was rarely more complicated than get set up and let myself hit it as well as I could. Unknowingly I learned to play golf by just doing it, like I learned to ride a bike, swim and pitch a baseball. In the ensuing years of growing up, marriage, family, career and now retirement, I have continued to enjoy my best results when I let myself just hit the ball and enjoy being out there.

However, I've seen many players whose skills and physical attributes are as good as or better than mine, but they don't seem to be willing to let themselves just hit it. They are always talking about this, that or the other mechanical thing they either forgot to do or didn't do well enough. They frequently don't seem to be having too much fun either. It aroused my curiosity. I wanted to understand why some players get better results out of their abilities while others, no matter how hard they work at it or physically talented they are, never seem to get much better.

The more I thought about it, the more it seemed that my dad's early instructions were pretty sound. My mind wasn't then nor is it now cluttered with a bunch of mechanical stuff and mental baggage every time I get ready to swing. I just did it, and I still just do it! After I get myself ready and set up I still try not to pay attention to anything but just hitting it!

My curiosity led me to research a continuum of golf instruction from Nicklaus to Harry Vardon's 1913 classic book, "How To Play Golf." My objective was to see how, over the years, greats of the game have "helped" us learn to play. The vast majority of instructional advice I have looked at, no matter how old or modern, seems to concentrate on all kinds of specific mechanical things and body positions. With very few exceptions there is not much written by great players about the role of their mind as they play golf. And yet interestingly they all seem to agree that the mental part of golf is at least 50% of successful performance.

It seemed to me that the two are inseparable so I set out to research the role of our minds when we play golf. I wasn't quite sure what I would find, but after piecing together countless random passages, anecdotes and the information I found in books and articles that probed the psychology of golf, I tried it out on myself. I was happily amazed that a very simple mental approach distilled from my research really helped my game. That is when I thought it might help others as much as it has me, and set out to write *The Simple Mental Secrets of Golf.*

In the evolution of my own game, I have learned to make the best of my changing abilities by continuing to let my body move as naturally as it can, and letting my mind work with, instead of against, my body. The result is that I have been able to maintain a single digit handicap from the "back tees" in spite of numerous operations on both of my hands over the last twenty years. After a couple years of research and writing I don't think it's naive to say that any golfer can improve by learning how a better golfing mind will let their bodies swing more naturally and intuitively whatever their skill level.

You were right, Dad, the best way is to just go hit it!

Introduction

Some players say of their golf: "It doesn't really matter if I play well or badly. I don't take the game that seriously. I only play for the fun of it." If you are one of these you know you are kidding yourself. You do take golf seriously, and you know it would be more fun if you played better. Don't deceive yourself. Playing your best golf is important to you, otherwise you wouldn't bother with it! If golfers didn't take it seriously, there wouldn't be so much anguish over the game. Clubs would not be slammed into the ground, smashed against trees, or sent flying through the air like little helicopters. Too many golfers are in love with the game but often hate the way they play it.

In a survey of PGA Tour players, answers to the question "What percentage of your game is mental and what percentage is physical?" ranged from 50% to 95% mental. It seems sensible to devote some of our practice time to working on a part of our game that accounts for at least half of our performance.

At all levels of ability and skill, I believe there awaits an opportunity to play better golf. Improving from your present level, whether you are a novice or low handicapper, will result from how well you use your mind to improve the preparation and execution of your physical shotmaking ability.

Our best golf is played only when we consistently focus our attention on *WHAT* we want to do rather than *HOW* we are going to do it. Our best golf can never be played mechanically. Our best golf will only be played when we learn to trust the instincts that control our ability to swing a club. Fortunately, the ability to improve is contained within our own bodies and minds. More satisfying golf results from learning how to swing a golf club simply and naturally with a well-prepared mind that is focused on *WHAT* we want to see happen.

A swing that works for you can be learned because there is nothing artificial or unnatural about learning what it feels like to sense and recognize your own body motion. You can also learn to combine your basic mechanical preparations with the power of your mind to let your swing happen naturally. With a swing that is natural to your body and good mental preparation, you can improve your game and increase your enjoyment of this wonderful pastime.

The number of good shots in each round depends entirely on how well you can blend together and manage your mechanical and mental skills. A novice player may hit only a few good shots each time out, but the satisfaction of feeling and seeing the results of a solidly struck ball feeds their golfing enjoyment just as much as it does players at the highest skill levels.

Golf, even at the highest levels of skill and competition, is a game of minimizing the number and the effects of missed shots and accepting a fairly large number of less than perfect shots. Misses can be minimized by learning to combine our physical and mental skills to prepare for and execute each shot and putt.

The best golfers in the world are the touring pros. In an even-par round, a pro rarely hits the ball solidly or lands it right on their target more than about 60% of the time. When shooting an under par round, solid hits and target accuracy may increase to 75% or so. On a bad day, solid shots and targets hit may be 40% or less of their total shots. On a good day pros rarely hit more than 80% of their drives in the fairway, hit less than 75% of the greens "in regulation," and only get the ball up and down in one putt from greenside bunkers about 60% of the time. Players who prevail at the end of the day are those who have made the most out of their missed shots.

Regardless of skill level, any golfer can reduce the incidence and severity of missed shots by learning to combine simple preshot preparations and natural swing mechanics with the awesome power of the mind. You will see how the shotmaking results produced by your golfing body are sensed and controlled by your golfing mind. Your golfing mind consists of what I call the *thinking mind* and the *sensing mind.* When you effectively apply both to your game, the result is better shots more often.

This book does not deal much with other mental elements of playing golf such as course management and strategy. Neither will it delve into the psychological bases of emotions, doubts, fears, anxieties, attitudes, confidence, self esteem, or positive thinking. These are topics for professional sports psychologists. *The Simple Mental Secrets of Golf* presents a practical and easily applied way for golfers of all skill levels to focus their minds on a preshot process and on their swing to get the most out of their natural abilities.

To help you most effectively use your mind when playing, I have reviewed the fundamental mechanics of the game. The intent is to help you develop an awareness of how *your* body feels and looks when *you* set up and *you* swing a golf club. The sections on grip, setup and swing are not intended to be instructional in the classic sense of how to do particular mechanical things. They are intended to provide guidelines to develop what works best for you. They are the sort of basic things that will let you "just go hit it."

To learn the fundamentals of playing golf from scratch, or improve some particular part of an ailing swing, there is no substitute for a capable PGA professional who is also a good teacher. Don't avoid seeking professional help whenever you think your game needs a tune-up or maybe even an overhaul.

The learning process in *The Simple Mental Secrets of Golf* focuses on six key elements of playing that have helped me and which I think will help you achieve your most consistent results. They are:

- **Learning how a proper grip feels and looks in your hands.**

- **Learning how a proper setup looks and feels to your body.**

- **Learning how the dynamic movements of a balanced swing feel to you .**

- **Learning and repeating a preshot preparation process.**

- **Learning to use your thinking mind without producing fear and muscle tension.**

- **Learning to use your sensing mind to get your body ready and make your swing.**

In my experience as a "recreational golfer," I have found that when I know *WHAT* I want to do and *HOW* it should feel to me, my whole mind works to improve my shotmaking results, my scoring, and my golfing enjoyment.

The Simple Mental Secrets of Golf

How To Make Them Work For You

I. MECHANICAL AND MENTAL GOLF

Golfers have a seemingly insatiable desire to improve their performance. From beginners to tour professionals, we are frequently dissatisfied with some part of our game. We often seem convinced that all it takes to make it better are one or more mechanical fixes. Often, to the detriment of our ball striking and scoring, we think and worry about how to improve our results by changing our grip, our setup or our swing mechanics. Also, thanks to aggressive and persuasive marketing, we are bombarded and often convinced that by merely acquiring the latest in high tech equipment, our play will miraculously improve.

Unfortunately, it seems we give too little thought to how we can improve our play with a better mental approach to our preparations and our shotmaking. It is, however, a demonstrated fact that our best athletic performances *only* occur when our minds are properly focused and in harmony with our physical mechanics.

The purpose of the next several chapters on the grip, the setup and the swing are not intended as new information in the already crowded library of mechanical golf instruction. My intent is to help you to recognize the importance of feeling these key mechanical elements as your body experiences them. They can then be embedded in and effectively used by your mind. I think it will help you bring them together in your mind to produce better shotmaking results with your body's natural ability. When your mind knows what you want your body to do and how it feels to you when you do it, you can better use its awesome power to improve your golf results.

To play golf we must all master a few mechanical skills to make up a swing. To play our best golf, no matter what our skill level, we must also learn to use our mind effectively. If we don't know how to use our mind power correctly, we will *never* play our best, no matter how mechanically sound our swing is or how physically and athletically talented we may be.

When we are playing golf, our mind uses its conscious and subconscious capabilities. Throughout the book, I characterize these capabilities as *thinking* and *sensing*. In my usage, *thinking* is deliberate mental activity. *Sensing* is that which takes over from our deliberate thinking, and with imagination and past experience, produces rhythm, intuition, muscle control, and what golfers call "touch."

Thinking

On the golf course, the thinking mind observes and analyzes the things that affect the conditions of play and the shotmaking options available. We think when we observe and analyze how the ball is lying, how wind conditions may affect the upcoming shot, what the expected distance is to our target and whatever hazards and obstructions must be accounted for and avoided. We think about shot possibilities and the feel of physical sensations in our hands and throughout our body as we grip the club and set up our body posture.

Unfortunately, many golfers also think about things that can go wrong such as hitting the ball into ponds, bunkers, trees, out of bounds, and so forth. They think about the mechanics of their swing. They worry about whether they will hit the ball off line or fail to hit it solidly. And they even get anxious about the score or worry about winning or losing a match or a bet. These and many other thoughts can be swirling around in their thinking minds when they are playing.

Negative thoughts generate *FEAR*. Fear produces muscle tension and stress throughout the body. Muscle tension and stress hinder the free movement and rhythm of our body and probably spoil more shots and putts than anything else we can do to our golf swing.

When we control fear and the resulting tension and stress, our bodies remain more relaxed and better able to make our most natural swings. Swing-spoiling muscle tension is greatly reduced. We all need to learn to eliminate or at least minimize thinking about things that produce the fear that interferes with our most natural swings.

Sensing

Sensing performs several functions in our golfing mind. It tells us if what we are doing physically and the decisions we are making seem and feel right or not. Our sensing mind "listens to" and "talks to" our thinking mind. If our sensing mind believes that things are okay, our thinking mind "hears" nothing. If something doesn't seem right to our sensing mind, it sends us a message. This is usually in the form of an uncomfortable feeling that something isn't quite right. To help us avoid making mistakes, this is our sensing mind's signal telling us to reconsider what we are thinking about or getting ready to do. You will learn to recognize and heed these signals as you play.

Our sensing mind will accept and assess whatever information we decide to feed into it. If we feed it with fearsome thoughts, doubts and anxieties, it will respond by tensing up muscles all over our body. If we feed it with objective, unemotional and non-judgmental information and observations we are seeing and thinking about, our body will stay more relaxed and can move more rhythmically and naturally.

When we let our sensing mind hear only objective, non-judgmental observations and unemotional assessments that are unclouded by fears and anxiety, our preparations and our shotmaking will improve. When it is not gripped with fear, it can help select the best club for the kind of shot we have chosen to play. It can help align our club and body toward the target. It can help us locate the lines on which our putt should travel. And it can select the spots on which our shots should land.

Sensing is a powerful but seldom used part of a golfer's mental ability. You will learn to use it to improve all your preshot preparations and your shotmaking results.

Sensing also combines with thinking to move all our body parts and swing the club. It motivates, controls and coordinates every part of our physical body. It blends all of our physical movements together to make up our swing. In short, sensing is the director in charge of our physical performance.

Using our sensing mind may be the single most important part of mental golf, but is probably the least understood. In perfect mental golf it works to execute our swing with *NO* thinking. Preshot preparations result from a combination of thinking and sensing. Our swing should result mainly from the work of our sensing mind.

When we make a golf swing, our mind should work a lot like it does when we return a tennis ball, shoot a basketball, or hit a baseball. To return a tennis serve, make a jumpshot, or hit a fastball, we must let our body move freely and naturally. We let it react instinctively. This produces the best results in any kind of athletic activity.

So it is with a golf swing. When we can shut out our thinking mind and let our sensing mind take charge of our swing, our bodies will move most naturally and our swing will happen most instinctively.

In the quest to play better mental golf, it can get a little scary in the beginning. This is because we must learn to entrust much of our preshot preparation and our entire swing to the hidden mystical power of our sensing mind. The way we use our mind as we play golf can help us hit good shots or it can sabotage our results. It is entirely up to each of us how much we allow our mind to help or to hinder our game.

There is a powerful relationship between our thinking mind, our sensing mind, our preshot preparations and the mechanics of our swing. The mental component of golf simply cannot be ignored if we expect to play our best. The more effectively we learn to manage our entire golfing mind, the better we will play, no matter what our skill level.

2.

THE "FEELINGS AND SENSES" OF GOLF

When we pick up a club, we feel it in our hands. We see how it looks as we are gripping it. When we set up to the ball, we feel how our body is positioned. When we swing the club, we feel our body moving. These are the sort of things I refer to as the "feelings" of golf — information that our mind uses to tell us that all is okay or that something is not quite right.

Unfortunately, far too often when making a golf swing or a putting stroke, players let stray thoughts distract their sensing mind. The resulting mishmash of mental activity will nearly always produce a poor shot or putt. The great golf teacher, Harvey Penick, once said: "The ability to concentrate one's mind is good, but thinking too much about how you are going to do what you want to do is disastrous. You must learn to trust your muscles to just hit the ball." That is the essence of swinging a golf club with a well-prepared mind.

When you learn how your basic swing and preshot elements look and how they feel, you can get your sensing mind working on your preshot preparations and on your swing. You will learn how to get your *whole mind* working to produce your best results. Paraphrasing Mr. Penick, you will learn just to hit the ball.

This won't happen automatically. You will need to experiment until you find grip, setup, alignment and swing "looks and feels" that work best for you. Learning to recognize the physical sensations and to visually recognize that which is effective will largely eliminate doubts about your preshot and swing preparations. Doubt breeds apprehension and anxiety, which, in turn produces fear. As we have seen, when fear is racing around in our golfing mind, muscle tension and stress develop. A poor shot is all but certain.

When you are confident and can recognize that your grip, setup, alignment and aim physically look and feel right, your mind will have far fewer preshot doubts. You can concentrate on letting your body naturally and instinctively make your swing. Learning how your preshot and swing mechanics look and feel is the first step in developing your best mental golfing ability.

Practice Makes Perfect

We cannot learn the feel and look of athletic movements just by studying descriptions and theories. We must experience and repeat them often enough until they become a part of our sensing mind's memory. In all learning experiences we do this by repeating actions and movements that produce successful results until we can easily recognize the feel of each and each seems normal. To maximize our golf results, there is no substitute for practicing what works.

When our golf "looks and feels" are right for us, solid ball contact with the ball heading for our target will happen more often. When you make a good shot, take some time to reflect on it. Replay the feel of the grip, the setup and the swing in your mind. Visualize how well and how far the ball flew. Immediately reviewing the feel and results of a good shot is a powerful way to improve your game.

How often have you hit a really good shot and then said to yourself, *how did I do that?* First try closing your eyes and replay the "feel and look" that produced the good results. Unless you have physically felt or mentally sensed something quite different from your "normal" swing don't try to figure out *HOW* it happened. Just replay and commit to your memory what *DID* happen. Your mind will file the experience away and you can later call on it to help you duplicate that good shot another time.

If you did detect something materially different in a swing that produced a great shot see if you can figure out what it was. If you can identify it make a few practice swings and try to recreate it's feeling before you hit your next practice ball. If you can't identify something pretty specific forget it. You probably just got lucky with one swing.

3.

HIT SOLIDLY AT THE TARGET

We are trying to achieve only two results when we hit a golf ball. We want to hit it solidly on the clubface and hit it toward a predetermined target. All kinds of different golf swings can produce solid ball contact with the ball heading in the desired direction. All we need to do is to have the clubhead moving at its maximum controllable speed when it strikes the ball and have the clubhead traveling straight toward the target. We can make just about any kind of swing we want to as long as these two things happen in the last few inches before impact.

From start to finish a complete golf swing takes from one to one and a half seconds or so. The time it takes for the club to travel from the top of the backswing to the end of the follow-through is just a few tenths of a second. There isn't time to think much about what is happening or to try to control and adjust various mechanical parts of our swing.

Basic Preparations

To consistently hit the ball solidly at their target all top players do four things, regardless of how their swings look in action.

- They *always* perform a particular preshot routine.
- They swing the clubhead through the ball at its highest *controllable* velocity.
- The clubface is *pointing* at their intended target line at impact.
- They *effectively* use their minds as they prepare themselves and execute each shot.

Anyone can learn to integrate their mind power into their preparations and the natural mechanics of their golf swing. However, to get the most out of your mental golfing ability you must also train your mind to recognize *how* your preshot preparations and *how* your swing mechanics look and feel to you. And, you must become very comfortable with them.

This is where learning to sense the feel of your preshot preparations and your swing can get complicated by popular theories of the day and the tips that are constantly offered to all golfers. Other than perhaps in surgical training, there seems to be more instruction in greater detail on how we're supposed to do all kinds of mechanical moves in our golf swing than in just about anything I can imagine. It doesn't seem that it ought to be that difficult.

Instruction and professional teaching clearly have an important place in learning to play. They can also be very helpful in analyzing and correcting faults. However, if allowed to clutter up your mind, the avalanche of mind-numbing "how to swing" details will generally produce the common condition known as *paralysis by analysis.*

Notwithstanding all the instructions and tips that are available, we really need to concentrate primarily on learning the key parts of our own preshot routine and the basic mechanics of our own swing. As we each learn our own preshot routine and swing mechanics, we will fine-tune the process to suit ourselves. We will combine and refine various parts to blend them into a process that works best for each of us.

If you persist, I believe you can learn to make a decent golf swing with no more thought than you focus on walking, shaking hands or brushing your teeth. Think about it. How much instruction do we seek out and practice in the techniques of walking, shaking hands or brushing our teeth? And yet, once we acquire the feel of moving our bodies to do these kinds of "natural" things, we do them and hundreds of other everyday activities without much thought at all about how we are doing them. We just let them happen. We just do them!

This is not intended to trivialize the difficulty of playing really good golf. Great players are wonderful athletes who make the very most of their physical and mental talents. The great players have learned to manage their bodies and their minds so they can, without fear, let themselves just hit it. I don't see any reason why anyone who wants to play golf their best can't also make the most of their natural talents. Is there any reason short of profound incapacity why anyone can't learn to let themselves just hit it?

You *can* teach your mind what preshot preparations and a natural swing should look like and feel like to you. You *can* embed these looks and feels in your mind. Then if you will just trust your mind to help you, you *can* swing the club naturally and instinctively the way your body wants to move.

Although the approach is simple there are no shortcuts. You must invest the time to build confidence that you are doing the right things for your body. If you are willing to work at it, you will be rewarded by making more solid ball contact with fewer mishit and misdirected shots. Let's start by looking at the basic mechanical elements of a preshot routine. They are:

- **How you grip the club.**
- **How you set up your body posture.**
- **How you aim the clubface and your body.**

Of these three mechanical preshot fundamentals, how you grip the club is the most important. When you have learned the feel and look of putting your hands on the club in a way that is right for you, you will have mastered at least 50% of the mechanical skill needed to hit the ball solidly. With a poor grip, you start right out behind the eight ball.

When balanced setup posture and accurate body alignment and club aiming are added to a good grip, you will be at least *80%* of the way to mastering the key mechanical skills needed to make a natural swing. A good grip combined with well-balanced posture and good alignment and aim will give your body the maximum opportunity to deliver the clubface squarely to the ball and make its most instinctive swing movements.

Because each person's physical makeup is different, every golfer develops a grip, setup posture and a swing that is uniquely their own. Accept the fact that your body will move and look different from some "classic" model because your physical attributes and abilities are different.

For example, the size, strength and the way your hands naturally hang will largely determine a grip with which you can best control the club. Your body's stature and configuration will largely determine your particular setup posture and the swing plane on which the club will naturally travel. Your flexibility and strength will determine the club head speed you can controllably generate while remaining well-balanced. Your basic hand-eye coordination will determine the timing, rhythm and tempo of your swing. In short, your swing will be unique just to you.

4.

MECHANICAL FUNDAMENTALS

Your Grip

Learning a grip that works for you is the single most important mechanical skill that you must master to play your best golf. It is the starting point on which everything else is built. When your grip is right, many faulty shots will simply be eliminated.

Because our hands are the only connection we have with the golf club, they must work together as well as possible to produce our most powerful and accurate shots.

In a golf grip, each hand has a distinct function. (Throughout the book, I will be describing things from a right-hander's viewpoint. For you lefties, remember to reverse the terms "left" and "right" as you read, and thanks for your patience.)

The job of the left hand is to secure and keep the club aimed so the clubface naturally returns squarely to the ball. The right hand delivers the hitting power through the shaft to the clubhead.

Our left hand is the most important of our two hands. If the left hand is not in position to naturally square up the clubface just before impact, all sorts of mishits are likely. There are two keys to a good left-hand grip. They are where and how the clubshaft is secured in your hand and where the clubface is pointing when your left hand is naturally gripping the club.

There are three commonly used ways to grip the club with your left hand. Probably the most popular and widely used is the "Vardon" overlapping style. There are also the interlocking style and the ten-finger or baseball style grips. With each of these grip styles the left thumb is extended a little right of center down the shaft toward the clubhead. An uncommon grip is described by a popular golf teacher in the early 1930s, Alex Morrison.

With the "Morrison grip," your left thumb is curled *under* the shaft and rests snugly against your middle finger that is curled in the opposite direction. Your left index finger remains off the shaft and relaxed to later interlock with the little finger of your right hand. In the Morrison grip, when your right hand is placed on the club, your little finger is interlocked between the left index and middle fingers. The lifeline pocket of your right hand rests on top of the left thumb. The remaining fingers and thumb of the right hand curl around the shaft the same way they do with the more conventional grips.

The Morrison grip does two things a little differently from a conventional left-hand grip. It seems to hold the club more securely with little chance for it to loosen or change position during the swing. And it frees the left wrist to hinge exactly the same and as freely on the downswing as the right wrist does on the backswing. For some players this may make it easier to control the club and for both wrists to uncock the club more smoothly and naturally through the hitting area.

I have tried it and found I can't comfortably interlock my little finger because of my surgically redesigned hands. However, even though it was a little uncomfortable, I felt I hit the ball a little farther with a little less effort than I did with my old faithful Vardon grip. With the latest revision to my right hand about healed up I think I'll try it again.

The next time you practice, give it a try. Once you have overcome the different feeling in your hands, you will notice a sense of freedom in both wrists that cannot quite be duplicated with a conventional grip. When your swing timing adjusts to this freer feeling, you may sense your club swings very smoothly through the hitting area. And when you get comfortable with it, you may even find that you also hit the ball straighter and perhaps even a little farther with less effort.

Whatever grip style you choose, learn how it feels and looks when a club is held in the *palm and fingers* of your left hand. You can see how this looks with the following easy test. Grip the club with both hands as you normally do and aim the clubface at an imaginary target. Then with your left hand still on the club, take your right hand away and raise the club until it points straight in front of you parallel to the ground. Turn your left hand up so you can see your fingers closed around the club shaft. With your right hand, grasp the club down the shaft a little way and firmly hold it so you can open your left hand without moving the club. Then open your left hand and look where the club shaft is lying. If you can see a little of your palm between the shaft and the base of your last three fingers, you have got it right. If you can't see some of your palm between the shaft and these fingers, you are gripping the club too much in your fingers.

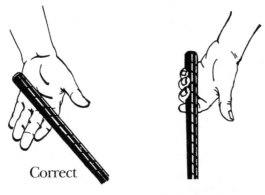

Correct

Incorrect

With a predominantly finger grip, the club will not be as secure, and it will be more difficult for your left hand to naturally return the clubface squarely to the ball.

Hand Position

Because each person's hands hang from their arms a little differently, you need to experiment with the position of your left hand on the shaft to get it just right for you. Your left hand will always try to return to its natural hanging position, even when it is swinging a golf club. You need to learn in what position your left hand should be on the club so it can naturally return the clubface squarely to the ball. Experimenting with left-hand positions and grip styles is the only sure way that you can get your grip correctly positioned for *your* left hand as it naturally hangs from the end of your arm.

To see how your hands naturally hang, stand erect with your shoulders, arms, wrists and hands completely relaxed at your sides. Then bend at the waist just enough so your hands hang a little in front of you. Look at your left hand and note where the space between your thumb and forefinger is pointing. My natural stance is shown on the left, my friend Al's on the right.

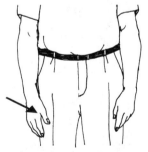 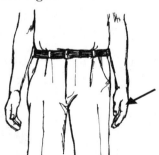

hanging inward   *hanging   square*

When hanging relaxed, most people's hands point more or less toward each other (left), but others' hang square. Exactly where your hands point when you are bent slightly at the waist and your arms are hanging relaxed is something you must figure out for yourself. When you know how your hands naturally hang, always try to put your left hand on the club shaft as close as possible to its naturally hanging position.

An easy way to get your left hand grip right for you is to start by letting your left arm hang relaxed against your side. Keeping your elbow comfortably against your side then raise your forearm so it points in front of you about parallel to the ground. Keep your forearm, wrist and hand relaxed. Grasp the club shaft near the bottom of the grip with your right hand and hold it upwards at about a 45 degree angle to your forearm and hand. Adjust the sole of the clubface so it is squarely facing an imaginary target line. This will be when the club sole is vertical relative to the ground.

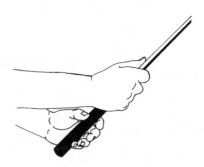

Keeping your wrist and hand completely relaxed press the grip lightly into your hand. Place the shaft so it rests against the middle joint of your index finger and under the heel pad of your hand.   Close your fingers around the shaft followed by your thumb curled *under the shaft.* Take your right hand away and position your thumb down the shaft for one of the conventional grips.

If you are trying the Morrison grip leave your thumb curled under the shaft. If your forearm, wrist and hand have stayed relaxed when you placed the club in your hand and closed your fingers and thumb around the shaft, the club will be squarely aligned. Practice this process and then make some swings to check it out in action.

There are a couple of dynamic ways you can check your left hand grip position and make adjustments to get it just right for you. The first involves making practice swings without a ball. The second involves observing the ball flight when you make a good swing and hit it solidly. Because your left hand grip is so important, it is a good idea to use both methods to assess the effectiveness of your grip in your practice sessions.

To use the practice swing approach grip a club and set up as you normally do. Without a ball, make a full practice swing. Then, with both hands still on the club and without moving either hand, return to your starting position and set the club back on the ground. If your grip is naturally squaring the clubface, it will still be pointing at your "target" when you set it back on the ground. If your left-hand grip is closing the clubface at impact, it will be facing a little toward you when you set it back down after your swing. If your grip is opening the clubface at impact, it will look just the opposite with the clubface pointing slightly away from you. If your grip does not naturally square up the clubface when you make a practice swing, you need to keep experimenting and adjusting it until you discover your left-hand position that consistently and naturally squares it up.

Another way to check your left-hand position is to observe the ball flight when you make a good swing and hit it solidly. If the ball curves too much to the left (a hook), the clubface is too closed at impact. Your left hand needs to be a little more toward the right on the shaft. If the ball curves too far to the right (a slice), the clubface is too open at impact. The remedy is to turn your hand a little farther to the left on the shaft. When the ball tends to fly pretty straight, or curve a little to the right (fade) or to the left (draw), that is the position in which your left hand naturally wants to be when it brings the clubface into the hitting zone a few inches from the ball.

Experimenting with slight adjustments to your left-hand position is the only sure way for you to get your grip right for your body. When you determine how your left hand must be placed on the club to hit the ball as you want, work on it until it has a feel and look you can easily sense and visually recognize every time you take your grip.

When your left-hand grip is right for you, it is easy to correctly position your right hand. Simply lay the "lifeline pocket" between the base of your thumb and heel of your right hand on top of your left thumb. Then lightly curl your fingers under and around the shaft.

Whether you prefer the overlapping Vardon grip, the interlocking little finger grip, the ten-finger grip or the Morrison grip, your left hand position will always be the same when your clubface is facing the target.

When gripping the club, you should sense that your palms are facing each other and your hands feel snugly and compactly fitted together. The feel of gripping with your left hand should be strong enough to firmly secure the butt of the clubshaft under the pad at the heel of your hand, but not so tight as to "choke" the club. The finger pressure in your right hand should be light and also be felt a little alongside the forefinger as it presses against the shaft. Finally, you should feel the lifeline pocket of your right hand pressing down a little on your left thumb.

Experiment with gripping pressures in each hand until you get a feeling that your wrists and forearms are relaxed and the club shaft is secure. Consciously check these feelings every time you take your grip. If you are willing to take the time to get your left-hand grip right for your body and your right-hand position worked out, everything else will be a whole lot easier.

Your Setup

A golf swing is a rhythmic athletic move. Your body setup is the key to swinging the club smoothly and powerfully in rhythmic balance. With practice, every golfer can develop a well-balanced athletic setup that best suits their body, their strength and their flexibility.

To get the feel of your setup, start by standing erect with the inside of your heels about shoulder width apart, your left foot pointed a little toward the target and your right foot pretty square to the target line. Then, keeping your back comfortably straight from your neck down and keeping your chin comfortably up, bend your upper body forward a little from the waist just until your arms can swing freely back and forth in front of you.

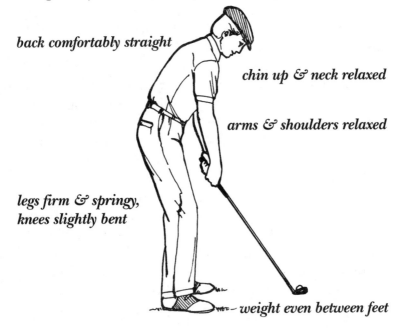

back comfortably straight

chin up & neck relaxed

arms & shoulders relaxed

legs firm & springy, knees slightly bent

weight even between feet

   As you bend from the waist, let your knees relax a little and your bottom move back a little so you feel your weight about evenly between your heels and the balls of your feet. You should feel little or no weight on your toes. In fact, you ought to be able to wiggle your toes up and down a little in your shoes without feeling unbalanced. Press your knees slightly toward each other until you feel a little weight on the inside of the ball and heel of each foot. With this basic setup, your body is in a balanced athletic posture that will let it move quickly and smoothly in any direction.

When you are in a well-balanced golf posture, your back will be comfortably straight, your chin will be up, your thighs and hips will have moved slightly back, your bottom will be sticking out a little and your arms, extended but relaxed, will be hanging naturally from your shoulders. You should feel firmly supported on the inside of your feet, feel a springy tension in your legs and feel a little stretching across the small of your back.

When your setup is complete, you should feel that your arms, shoulders and torso are relaxed while your feet and legs are firm, springy and ready to move. Your hip area should feel neutral, neither quite as relaxed as your upper body nor as firm as your lower body.

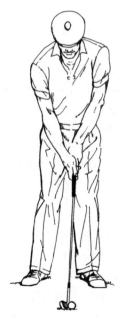

upper body relaxed

lower body springy

In a balanced golf posture, you'll look a little like an infielder or linebacker just before a play starts. The similarity is that you, the infielder and the linebacker will be set to move smoothly and powerfully. The differences are that you will be standing a little taller and, of course, will be holding a golf club.

Practice getting into your setup in front of a mirror. Observe how your body looks and sense the physical feelings in your legs, waist, back and shoulders. Make a mental picture of how all of this looks and feels and commit it to your memory every time you practice getting into your setup.

Your Aim

The key to aligning your body and eyes as you set up is to always aim the clubface before you aim your feet and the rest of your body. Start by getting your left hand on the club, followed loosely by your right hand. With your feet fairly close together, position the clubface on the target line. When your clubface is lined up, keep it there and align your feet and body by moving around until you sense that they are parallel to the target line. With your club still aimed, establish the width of your stance and your distance from the ball.

One way to aim your club is to pick out a spot such as a leaf, twig, or spot on the grass a few feet or so in front of the ball and directly on your target line. As you move into your setup, keep your eyes on your aiming spot, drawing an imaginary line from the aiming spot through the ball a few inches. Point the clubface squarely down your imaginary target line. Then move your feet into your setup position while you keep the clubface aimed and your eyes on your target line. After you have aimed the clubface and your feet, *then* adjust your right-hand grip on the club. This sequence of left-hand grip, aim the club, set up your feet, then adjust your right-hand grip will go a long way to eliminating many misdirected shots. Experiment with variations until you find an aiming process that works best for you and then stick with it.

Your Body and Eye Alignment

To get your body aligned, move your torso around until you sense your shoulders, hips and the front of your thighs are parallel to your aiming line. When you sense your body is on the target line, align your eyes. Your eyes *must* be on the target line because your body, and thus your swing, will tend to move on whatever path your eyes are seeing.

Getting your body and eyes aligned is a job your sensing mind should do for you. First visualize and retain a picture of the aiming line in your mind's eye. Then let your body move around until you sense that your feet, hips, shoulders and eyes are parallel to the line. This may seem a little strange at first, but if you have picked a target and sense that your clubface is accurately aimed at it, you will learn to trust your mind to move your other parts around until they too are lined up. Finally, when you are finished setting up your posture and lining yourself up, put it all out of your mind and pay no further attention to any part of your setup.

Between the completion of your setup and alignment and the beginning of your swing, try to keep loose by moving one or more parts of your body a little to prevent the buildup of pre-swing tension. For example, you might rock slightly from side to side on your feet, wiggle your toes, or make smooth waggles of the club along the target line. Whatever you do to keep loose don't think about it. Just do it! Watch the pros and see how many of them keep a little body movement going until just before they swing.

Review

Your Grip:
- **Left-hand on the club in its natural hanging position.**
- **Palms facing each other.**
- **Left-hand pressure in palm and last three fingers.**
- **Right-hand lifeline pocket pressing on left thumb.**
- **Right forefinger contacting the club shaft.**
- **Forearms and wrists relaxed.**

Your Setup:
- **Firm, springy feeling in feet and legs.**
- **Inside of heels shoulder width apart.**
- **Back comfortably straight and chin up.**
- **Knees relaxed and bottom sticking out a little.**
- **Weight even between both feet.**
- **Weight even between heel and ball of each foot.**
- **Weight a little on the inside of each foot.**
- **Relaxed upper body and neutral hips.**

Your Aim:

- **Both eyes on the aiming spot as you approach the ball.**

- **Draw an imaginary line from the aiming spot through the ball.**

- **Aim the clubface before setting your feet.**

Your Body and Eye Alignment:

- **Shoulders, hips and thighs parallel to the aiming spot line.**

- **Both eyes parallel to the aiming spot line.**

- **Stay loose before your swing starts.**

As you develop a complete preshot routine, the mechanical parts of your preparation will combine into a smoothly flowing process that you will do before every shot–from your first drive to your last putt. To incorporate the feelings of a correct grip, good posture, accurate club aiming and body alignment into your sensing mind, you must practice combining them until they become a series of natural things that blend together before every shot. Only when your preshot routine feels natural and seems to *just happen* will you have confidence that you have prepared yourself to make your best swing.

Remember, when you get your grip and setup right, you will be at least 80% of the way to making your best mechanical swing. Work on them until they feel comfortable and natural. You'll know you've got it right for yourself when you seem, without much thinking, to settle naturally into a grip and a setup whenever you see a golf ball waiting to be hit.

5.

FEELING A BALANCED SWING

Of the hundreds and perhaps

even thousands of muscle and joint movements in a golf swing, there are three key actions that blend everything else together. They should be practiced and repeated until you learn how each feels to your body. They are:

- **Turning your upper body.**
- **Turning your hips and working your legs.**
- **Keeping your arms relaxed and letting them swing in response to your turning body.**

These three body actions, when made with a good grip, from a balanced athletic setup posture and done in a rhythmically continuous motion, will produce a smooth flowing swing when you let them happen naturally.

Although this may seem a little too simple, given all that is written about how to make a golf swing, these basic actions are essentially all there is to it. In a balanced setup posture, learn how it feels to turn your upper body and hips around your spine, to brace the back leg and foot firmly and to swing your arms back and up for the backswing. Then learn how it feels to drive your legs and turn your hips and upper body back around toward the target and to let your relaxed arms seem to fall down and through the hitting area. And finally learn how it feels when you blend them all together into one continuous rhythmical movement. Remember: a golf swing is not a series of individual parts and positions — it is a continuous motion from start to finish.

Feeling Your Backswing

There are two distinct parts to the feel of a backswing. One is a growing firmness in your torso across your stomach and the other is a strong sense of coiling around the inside of your firmly braced back leg and foot.

To sense the feel of your legs and upper body, start by standing erect, but comfortably relaxed, in front of a mirror so you can see your whole body. Cross your arms loosely over your chest as you face the mirror. The inside of your arms should rest loosely, but noticeably, against the sides of your chest. In this position your body's center of mass is in about the middle of your torso near your stomach. This is the place in your body where your swing movement is centered and around which all your other parts naturally tend to move.

Your first sense of backswing movement is in your upper body. This is in your upper back and shoulders. If your hips stay relaxed, they will also turn with your upper body and shift your weight to your back foot. Although there is a slight delay between the beginning movement in your upper body and the subsequent movement of your hips and legs, you want all of these parts to *feel* like they are flowing in a smoothly, continuous rhythmical motion. As your upper body turns, keep the inside of your upper left arm lightly against the outside of your chest and keep your arms relaxed. This is what is meant by the so-called "one piece takeaway." Your whole body — from your legs to your shoulders — feels as if it is coiling up in one continuously smooth motion.

Turn your body around a firmly braced back leg until you feel the muscles across your stomach become firm. This is a key swing feel. If you force yourself to turn farther, you will begin to sway your head and shoulders away from the turning axis of your spine and the support and bracing provided by the inside of your back leg and foot. Keep your chin up and your neck relaxed as you turn back. By keeping your neck relaxed, your head can move a little and still remain generally centered on your spine. A relaxed neck acts like the gimbals of a ship's compass. It allows your head and your eyes to stay level and focused on the ball and the target line throughout all the other backswing motions.

When you feel resistance to turning farther, you will see that your hips have turned a little less than your shoulders. Do not force either your shoulders or hips to turn farther than they naturally want to turn. When your hips are fully turned for your body, you will feel the muscles on the outside of your front thigh begin to firm up a little and you will sense a strong feeling of being solidly braced by firm muscles on the inside of your back leg and foot. When your shoulders are fully turned, you will feel a stretchy firmness across your back.

Repeat your backswing exercise, but this time begin with your body in a balanced setup posture with your arms still crossed over your chest. As you turn back, feel the firmness on the outside of your front thigh and a sense of bracing on the inside of your back leg, particularly inside the ball of your foot and heel. Remember to keep your chin up and your neck relaxed as your body turns.

In the last phase of your backswing exercise, get your arms and hands fully involved by letting them hang comfortably with your palms loosely together in a simulated grip and your body in a balanced setup posture. Turn your body, starting in your upper back and shoulders. With the inside of your upper left arm staying relaxed and in contact with your chest, let your hands swing back and up as your body turns away from the "target." Don't intentionally pick your arms or hands up. Keep them relaxed and let them swing naturally. Notice that your arms and hands will rise nearly to your shoulders, without much additional effort on your part. As your arms swing back and up, you may also notice your left elbow bends a little. Don't worry about it as long as your upper arm stays relaxed and riding against your chest. It will straighten out when it needs to at the bottom of your swing.

As you practice turning your body and swinging your arms in front of a mirror, watch your chin. See your upper body turning around your spine and back leg while your head, sitting atop your relaxed neck, remains fairly level even though it moves back and forth and maybe even up and down a little. Feel your arms staying very relaxed. Feel the coiling around the inside of your back leg. And feel your weight being braced on the inside of your back foot between the ball and the heel.

When you practice the feel of your backswing, run through the entire sequence several times, always starting from an athletic setup posture. Focus your mind and sense the feel of starting your backswing in your upper body, keeping your upper left arm lightly in contact with your chest and continuing to "the top of your swing." Make a few rhythmic backswings with your eyes closed. This will enhance the feelings of smoothness, balance and bracing.

Feeling Your Downswing

When you can feel the buildup of energy in your backswing, then learn how it feels to smoothly release it in a downswing. After a full backswing, start your downswing by turning your hips toward your front leg, followed in order by your upper body, then your arms, hands and the club. Finish standing fairly erect on your front leg with the outside of your heel and foot facing your imaginary target. Don't consciously pull your arms down but feel them lagging behind your turning body and falling, rather than being pulled. Also feel how your weight automatically shifts from the inside of your back foot and leg to the outside of your front foot and leg as you uncoil your hips and upper body back around to face your "target."

As your weight shifts from your back to your front foot, your turning hips and upper body will pass through an intermediate stage where your weight is about even between both of your feet. Run through a downswing slowly and watch your lower body as you turn toward the target. Notice your knees separating a little and notice the sensation in your lower body — your hips and legs — of slightly sitting down as you turn and your weight moves to your forward leg. Don't accentuate this. Just let it happen naturally. Then repeat the whole sequence until you feel you have embedded the sense of this key feeling in your mind.

Feeling a Complete Swing

To put the feel of your backswing and downswing exercises together, start from a balanced setup posture with your arms crossed loosely over your chest. Smoothly make a complete backswing, then a downswing. In your backswing, sense the turning and bracing feelings. As your hips and upper body turn forward on the downswing, sense the feeling of slightly sitting down as your shoulders and crossed arms start moving a little behind your torso and hips. Feel your crossed arms staying relaxed as they move a little slower than your shoulders. Try to feel this slightly delayed sequence of relaxed arms being a little slower than your shoulders, and your relaxed shoulders a little slower than your torso and hips. This is where the whip-like centrifugal energy that produces clubhead speed is developing.

Complete your full-swing exercise by assuming a balanced setup posture and extending your arms and hands into a simulated grip. Keep the inside of your left arm lightly against your chest and keep the arms relaxed throughout your swing. As your hands near the end of your backswing, notice the feeling of a little weight building on your front foot near your heel. This is your body's preparation for the downswing.

At this point your body is actually moving in two directions at once. Your hips and legs have begun to drive forward and turn toward your target while your upper body and the club continue to move back and up a little farther. Before your hands have reached the end of your backswing, your front foot and leg are already firming up and getting ready to support your upper body and arms when they turn forward and release their stored up energy.

When your downswing is complete, you should be balanced on the outside of your front foot and heel, your back should be comfortably erect and your belt buckle should be facing the target. Should you end up way out on the toes of your front foot, your shoulders and arms have probably moved too fast and your arms have tensed up and been "muscled" into the hitting area. The result is you have started to lose your balance and your toes are trying to keep you from falling over! Slow down and relax your arms and shoulders.

As your downswing gathers momentum, centrifugal force acting on the clubhead rapidly increases. When your left arm has fallen to where it is pointing at the ground a little behind your back foot, the clubhead is still far behind in your cocked hands. As your left arm continues swinging toward the ball, the clubhead quickly accelerates like the kid at the end of a "crack the whip" line. This acceleration produces tremendous centrifugal force that naturally uncocks your wrists. The result is an explosion of clubhead speed through the ball.

Pros and top amateur players often have the clubhead traveling over 100 mph in the hitting area. The clubhead speed of most recreational golfers is in the 60 to 90 mph range. Remember, from the top of your swing through the point of ball contact takes only a few tenths of a second. There is clearly not time to be thinking about various mechanical swing moves and trying to make conscious adjustments.

Feeling Your Natural Swing

When you pace your whole swing rhythmically, the individual mechanical parts will blend together and happen naturally. When you start from a balanced setup, your feet, knees and legs will support and promote your body turn without any conscious thinking or extra effort on your part. Prove this by watching your legs in the mirror as your body turns and your arms swing up. On the backswing, see your front knee naturally move in toward the imaginary ball position. The heel of your front leg may or may not lift a little off the ground. Don't intentionally pick it up but don't force it to stay down either. Just let it do whatever it wants to do. Particularly notice how your back leg stays bent a little at the knee but feels coiled and firmly braced against the inside of your foot. This is a key feeling and is essential to making the rhythmical hip and leg moves that control your downswing.

bent knee & leg firm   *knee & leg relaxed*

Imprint in your mind the image and feel of your body turning back around your slightly bent and firmly braced back knee and foot. As your relaxed arms rise to your shoulders, see how your wrists and hands, even without a club, tend naturally into a slightly cocked position when they get about shoulder height. When you are swinging a club the level to which your arms will rise, and the amount your wrists will naturally cock increase with the momentum of the moving club.

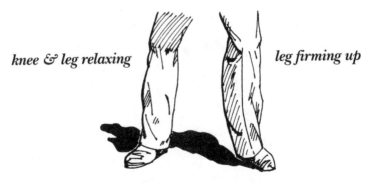

knee & leg relaxing   *leg firming up*

Sitting down feeling

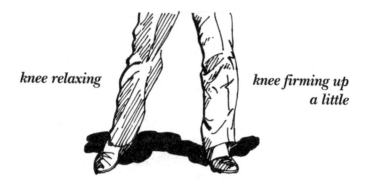

knee relaxing

*knee firming up
a little*

As your body turns through the hitting area, notice how your back leg naturally begins to relax after impact and turn toward the target, while your front leg takes on the job of bracing your forward turn and your follow-through. As your swing moves through the impact area, sense the feeling of your relaxed arms falling toward the ground and your weight moving from your back foot toward the outside of your front foot.

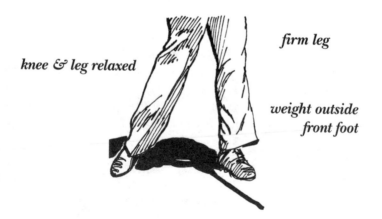

firm leg

knee & leg relaxed

*weight outside
front foot*

All of this will happen quite naturally and produce the rhythmic sequence of backswing and downswing angles, movements, and weight shifts that add up to your natural swing.

When you can swing a club through a backswing and downswing sequence without feeling jerkiness in your shoulders, arms and hands, you will have the feeling of "swinging within yourself." It is a feeling you sense when your body and the club are moving with a rhythm and speed that your muscles can readily control. If you swing too fast, your muscles will lose control of your body. Your balance will wobble around and the timing and rhythm of your swing will be thrown off. When your balance, timing and rhythm are out of whack, a mishit is a virtual certainty.

Swinging at less than your maximum speed is often called "staying (or swinging) within yourself." For some this is very hard to do. Many golfers have a mistaken notion that distance results from making a lusty swing at the ball. It doesn't! Distance results from the club reaching its maximum speed just a few inches from the ball. If your arms tense up and your shoulders move too fast relative to the rest of your body, you will never develop your maximum clubhead speed when the club reaches the ball. You will always hit the ball farther and more accurately when you learn to keep your shoulders and arms relaxed and swing within yourself.

You can get the feel of your ideal swing effort by simply trying different swing speeds and relaxed arm feels until you find a comfort zone where you have a sense of solid balance and good club control all the way through a swing that makes solid ball contact. When practicing, strive to maintain a feeling of relaxation, well-balanced smoothness and rhythm throughout your swing. If you sense tension while you are swinging, work on loosening it up. When you are right on, it feels almost effortless.

It might help to visualize your golf swing as being similar to hitting a nail on the head with a hammer. A strong, accurate hammer blow starts with a relaxed arm falling towards the nail with the hammer still cocked in your hand. As your arm nearly reaches the nail your wrist rapidly uncocks and — pow! — you hit it dead center. If you speed up, tense up or get jerky with your arm swing, your muscles are less able to control the rapidly moving hammer and a mishit is almost certain. Does this sound a little like the results you sometimes get when your arms and shoulders tense up and are moving a little too fast and get jerky? If so, you need only to slow down and relax your shoulders and arms to recover the balance and rhythm of your swing.

Hitting the Ball

When you understand the feel and look of a good grip, posture, aim, alignment and the basic swing mechanics, there is one more mechanical part of your swing that is the payoff for everything else. That is how your hands work to hit the ball. This is what the great Scottish golfer Tommy Armour called "the art of hitting with the hands."

The function of your hands is to guide and whip the clubhead through the ball. Your left hand controls the direction the clubface is pointing at impact. Your right hand transmits the final explosive clubhead speed. Through your right hand is where your body finally releases the energy to the clubhead and hits the ball.

When you make a well-balanced, rhythmic swing, you can choose how you want to let your hands move to hit the ball. You can let the downswing proceed naturally to impact entirely of its own accord. Or, as you refine control of your swing, you can supply additional "punch" in the hitting area by learning to feel a delay in the release of your wrists and hands as long as possible.

In the first approach, your wrists will uncock naturally as centrifugal force in the clubhead overcomes their resistance and snaps them back to the same position they were in when you addressed the ball. The natural uncocking of your wrists will produce plenty of clubhead speed to hit the ball a goodly distance.

Although letting your wrists uncock naturally is the easiest and most foolproof way to hit the ball, you also ought to try hitting it with extra punch when you practice. As the rhythm, timing and control of your downswing improve, you can hit the ball a little harder by learning how it feels to accelerate your right hand at just the right time to add a little more clubhead speed to any given shot.

You can get the feeling of adding extra punch to a shot by making half swings without a ball. Start with a good grip and assume a balanced setup posture without a ball. Make enough of a backswing to get your left arm up about waist-high. Your wrists will naturally cock, and the club will be roughly vertical to the ground. Then with relaxed arms, smoothly make a downswing and intentionally uncock your right hand through the imaginary hitting area when the club has swung down where it is about parallel with the ground. With this abbreviated swing, you will feel your right hand whip the clubhead strongly through the hitting area. You will also hear the characteristic swish of the club as it speeds by. Do this in slow motion a few times. Then gradually speed up until you feel you are letting your right hand hit *hard* through the ball with good balance and rhythm.

When you have made several smooth half-swings and can feel and hear the punch, try hitting a few balls. This will add the feel of making contact and swinging *through* the ball. After a little practice, you will be pleasantly surprised how solidly you hit it and also how far and how straight it flies!

Gradually work up to hitting a full swing with punch. As your confidence improves, add hitting half, three-quarter and full shots to your practice sessions. Even if you never add extra punch to a full shot while you are playing, a short swing with punch can frequently get you out of trouble.

Rhythm

Rhythm is the heart of every golf swing. Rhythm paces, times and integrates all the mechanical elements of the swing. We each have a natural rhythm that times and coordinates all of our body's movements. Our swing rhythm controls the timing and coordination of all our swing movements. If the natural pace of our rhythm is out of sync with the rest of our body because of tension or swinging "too hard," we sacrifice balance and club control. Poor balance and poor club control reduce the frequency of making solid contact, reduce clubhead speed and reduce how accurately and how far we will hit the ball.

Because each person's natural rhythm is unique to their body, you need to experiment with your swing speed until you get the feel of a speed that feels the most effortless, produces the most frequent solid ball contact and hits the ball the most accurately. In order of importance, your golfing objectives are first to hit the ball solidly and accurately, followed by increasing the distance of your shots.

You can nearly always make a good score on almost any golf course with a swing that hits the ball solidly and accurately even though your distance isn't as long as others. Even a somewhat wimpy shot that is safely in the fairway is better than a boomer that goes out of bounds, into the trees, the lake, or some other undesirable place. Your most rhythmic swing will produce a sense of maximum club control and most consistently result in the best distance and accuracy for your body.

If you are like most golfers, this will be a swing speed that feels slower than you are used to. It may seem so slow that you just can't believe you'll even hit the ball out of your own shadow! In his book *Tempo,* Al Geiberger writes: "By swinging slowly and easily, you will be in control of your swing. Your timing will be much better and you will develop a lot more clubhead speed than if you flail at the ball. You might be amazed at how well and how far you hit it."

One way to get the feel of your most rhythmic swing speed when you practice is to take a deep breath and then swing the club before you exhale. Holding your breath while swinging keeps the center of your body mass firm for a few seconds. This will tend to produce a smoother rhythm in your hips and lower body. With a little practice you will soon begin to get a feel for the rhythm that works best for your body.

With good swing rhythm, your arms remain relaxed until they reach the hitting area and your wrists uncock naturally or until you add extra punch to the shot. The keys to keeping your arms and hands relaxed on the downswing are good balance and how smoothly and rhythmically your legs, hips and upper body work.

When the unwinding sequence of the downswing is done rhythmically and with good balance, you will sense a smooth gathering of momentum in your upper body without feeling sudden or jerky movements in your shoulders, arms or hands. As your downswing begins in your hips and legs, your relaxed arms will follow your shoulders and feel as if they are falling toward the ground without any effort to hurry them along. One way to do this is simply ignore your upper body throughout your swing. In other words, don't think *swing* or *hit* or pay any attention to your shoulders, arms and hands. Work hard on developing a sense of smooth rhythm in your lower body and get the feel of keeping your shoulders and arms relaxed and letting your hands come along for the ride.

Learning Key Swing Feels

We must physically experience the feeling of doing each preshot activity and swing movement to embed the *feel of our body* in our sensing mind. Try the following practice method to help you reinforce the feel of your grip, setup and swing moves. You can use it while you are away from the course as well as on the practice range. When you have repeated the moves often enough to recognize your key swing looks and feelings, you can even practice entirely in your mind while relaxing in an easy chair or just about wherever you may be!

Away from the course, all you need for a little practice is you and a mirror. If you have the room, you can use a club — but be careful of the lamps. To practice in your mind, all you need is you! It only takes a few minutes to run through an entire practice session, including all the key preshot and swing parts. Whenever you practice — at home, at the range or wherever you are — perform each preshot and swing element several times before moving on to the next one. Think about each of them by seeing the look and sensing the feel of your body.

For example, do several grip practices, starting each time by selecting a club. Check the feel of your left-hand palm and finger relationship and see how your hand is positioned on the club every time you take a new grip. Set your body up in a balanced posture and make several backswing, downswing and complete swing moves. When you have done each individual backswing and downswing exercise several times, then string together some complete swings, starting with your setup and grip and ending by facing an imaginary target at the end of your "swing." The more you work on grooving the feel of your grip, setup and swing, the better your sensing mind will be at recognizing and instinctively performing each when you play.

When you practice on the range, always take a few minutes during your warm-up to run through your preshot and swing exercises a few times before you start to hit balls. Pay particular attention to sensing your natural rhythm. It changes from day to day — just as moods do! Check each of your key preshot and key swing feels. If, during your practice session, you sense your swing doesn't feel right, stop hitting balls for a few minutes and refresh your mind by running through your preshot and swing exercises a few times. When you do this, focus your mind on feeling the muscle and tactile sensations as you take your grip, set up your body in a balanced posture, and make your backswing and downswing moves.

By now you may be saying, "If my whole game has to change just to play better mental golf, forget it." Not to worry! Chances are you may not have to change very much at all. You may need only to practice a few simple checkpoints to embed the looks and feels that work the best for your body. For relatively little effort, the payoff of playing better golf is potentially great.

When you have confidence in your preshot routine, and you have no discomforting feelings, your sensing mind is saying you are ready to make a swing. If you are not so confident, but can't quite put a finger on the source of your discomfort, run through your checklist of preshot feels.

Once your sensing mind knows what everything should feel like to your body, it will let you know — with a vaguely uncomfortable feeling — if something isn't quite right. When heeded, this "warning" will give you another chance to regrip or reaim, or redo whatever else doesn't feel quite right before you launch off into your swing.

The same thing is true for your swing feelings. Much of what you already do in your swing may be right on the mark. But if something feels a little jerky or you are just not making solid contact, take a look at your rhythm and see if your arms are staying relaxed. Then take some time to revisit the other key checkpoints of your swing.

The reason to work on getting your mechanical preshot and swing feels right is to develop confidence that you are fully prepared to swing the club. Only when you are confident can you successfully turn your swing over to your sensing mind to make your shot. When your mechanical "golf feels" are in good order, you are well on your way to learning how to play your best mental golf. When you need a little more work to reinforce confidence in the look and feel of your game, the checkpoints and exercises will help you quickly restore a sound swing. They will also pave the way for your mind to get effectively involved in your swing. Confidence in your preshot preparations and your swing will give your sensing mind the maximum chance to help your body hit good shots.

Review

Backswing:

- **Upper body first to turn back with the inside of your upper left arm lightly against your chest.**

- **Hips, torso, shoulders, arms, hands and the club feel they are moving together.**

- **Shoulders, arms and wrists relaxed.**

- **Back leg firmly bracing your upper body turn.**

- **Neck relaxed and chin up.**

Downswing:

- **Hips and legs drive and turn forward.**

- **Feel your lower body sitting down a little.**

- **Shoulders, arms and hands feel relaxed and falling toward the ground.**

- **Feel your weight moving to the outside of your front foot and heel.**

In the next section we will explore a step by step approach you can use to develop a preshot routine that works the best for you. When you are satisfied with your preshot routine, then you will be ready to use your sensing mind to perform your swing.

6.

BUILDING YOUR PRESHOT ROUTINE

A preshot routine is where we do all of our thinking about the shot and where our observations, analyses and assessments are fed into those parts of our mind that do the sensing work. A preshot routine programs our mental computer. It makes it aware of the conditions we think will affect the shot and tells it what kind of shot we want to play and how we want it to turn out.

A preshot routine shifts attention away from our surroundings and our companions and prepares our body and our mind to make the upcoming shot. A preshot routine "programs" the body and mind. Its purpose is to get our sensing mind confidently prepared and committed to the shot before we swing. You are encouraged to develop your own routine. Try to include some version of each element and repeat each one *exactly* the same way before you make every shot.

During the preshot routine, we narrow the focus of our thinking mind and sharpen the concentration of our sensing mind. Then just before we begin to swing, we can confidently turn our body completely over to our sensing mind. The individual elements of a preshot routine organize and focus our attention with a logical and confidence-building process. The time to run through an entire preshot routine takes less than a minute. In this very short time frame before each shot, we concentrate our full attention *only* on preparing for the upcoming shot.

For maximum effect, a preshot routine should include each of the following elements in some form every time you get ready to make a new shot — from your opening tee shot to your final putt. The basic elements of a typical preshot routine include:

- **Focusing your mind on the present.**
- **Assessing the play possibilities and conditions.**
- **Deciding on the kind of shot you want to play.**
- **Committing to the selection of a club.**
- **Making practice swing(s) and getting your left hand grip set.**
- **Envisioning the shot results you want.**
- **Envisioning an aiming spot.**

- **Aiming your club.**
- **Setting up in a balanced posture and aligning your body and your eyes.**
- **Completing your grip and keeping your body loose.**
- **Refreshing your target image.**

Let's take a brief look at each of these to get a feel for the role each plays in the upcoming shot and how you can make them work best for you.

Focusing Your Mind on the Present

Between shots you can visit with your companions, act up and have all the thoughts you want, but as you approach the spot where your ball is lying you must start getting ready to play a golf shot. The *only shot* that you can do anything about is the one you are about to play. The shot at hand cannot be affected by any other shot you have previously played or any shot you will play later. You have only one job right now: getting your mind focused only on the shot you are getting ready to make.

Forget about previous bad shots, bad breaks or bad scores. Do not think or fret about holes and shots that you haven't even played yet. If you have just made a poor score on the last hole, you may still be a little hot under the collar. However, by the time you get to the next tee or wherever your next shot is, you must have completely put aside all your "mad emotions." You must get your mind settled so it can concentrate only on making your next shot.

On the other end of the emotional spectrum, if you have just made a great shot or score, you may be feeling pretty good. You need to stabilize an emotionally high state of mind the same as when you are unhappy or upset. The important thing is to try to keep your emotional state from getting too nonchalant, mad, elated or discouraged. Work on keeping your emotions as calm as you can.

At first it won't be easy to forget that crummy shot or bad break or whatever got you stirred up. If you need to, go ahead and beat yourself up a little or blame the golf gods or your club for your misfortune if you think it will make you feel better. It probably won't. If you need to celebrate a little, by all means do so. It is perfectly okay to work yourself over or celebrate a little. Just be sure you put it all completely out of your mind before you start your next preshot routine.

About the best way to handle a disappointing shot or other mishap is simply to tell yourself that you did your best. Remind yourself that every golf shot doesn't always turn out just as you wanted it to. If that isn't much comfort, remind yourself that you can't do anything about it anyhow! It's a done deal. It is a single, completely isolated event, the results of which can never be changed.

Unless you let it, a previous disappointment or elation will have absolutely no effect on how you play your next shot. The success of all your other shots will depend *only* on how well you prepare for and play each of them, one at a time. Focus your attention on what you can do now rather than what could have been. Save all that for the nineteenth hole when your round is over.

As you improve your ability to accept the bad shots with the good, it will be easier to focus your mind on the present before each new shot. You will also begin to even out your emotional highs and lows. You will operate mentally and emotionally on a more even keel throughout your round. The pros often call this "getting in the here and now." It is the essential first step in your preshot routine.

When you approach your next shot and have calmed your mind, the process of focusing your concentration begins. When you reach your ball you must be totally focused on the present and, with a clear mind, ready to prepare yourself to make the next shot. This is when you put aside the banter with your playing companions and begin to prepare your mind and your body for the upcoming shot.

The next three preshot jobs involve thinking about and assessing the playing conditions, deciding on the kind of shot you want to make and selecting the club you want to use.

Assessing Your Play Possibilities

Before you can select a club, you need to let your sensing mind know about the conditions you think are going to affect your shot. You also have to decide what kind of shot has the best chance of success. And you have to be honest with yourself about your shotmaking ability. Unless a match, or something equally important, is riding on the upcoming shot, don't overreach your ability by trying a shot you don't know how to play well or in which you don't have much confidence.

If you have a good lie in the fairway, you may have the best of all worlds. But if you are in the trees or have a poor lie or have obstructions to work around or over, your opportunities are probably more limited. Your key decision is to select a shot that, when honestly and objectively considered in light of your skill, has the best chance to be successful.

Whenever you are faced with a really tough or low percentage situation, it's almost always better to take your medicine and play the safest shot that will get you back into a good position. Give yourself the best chance to make a successful recovery shot. Rather than adding an extra stroke or two by trying some heroic shot out of the deep rough, the bushes or the trees, give yourself a chance to save a good score. Too often we try to make a spectacular play only to wind up worse or no better off for our next shot. This may test your patience a little but try not to sabotage your emotional state, your score or your chance to win or tie a hole by choosing a low percentage shot with big penalties for failure.

Regardless of the kind of shot you decide on, the only reason for assessing the possibilities and conditions of play is to choose the club best suited to make that particular shot. This is a job your sensing mind should do.

Start by evaluating and assessing the playing conditions non-judgmentally. In other words, just look at how your ball is lying and make yourself objectively aware of it. Don't make a big deal of a good lie or a bad lie. Merely take note of the fact that it is sitting down in the rough, is in an old divot or is sitting up beautifully just waiting to become a perfect shot. Do the same thing with the other conditions you are checking out too, such as the distance you want the shot to fly, how the wind speed and direction feel and any obstructions and hazards that need to be taken into account. Talk to your mind objectively about the conditions *as they exist* without judging them to be good or bad, fair or unfair.

This mental conversation will feed the information you are thinking about and observing into your sensing mind. The non-judgmental recognition of conditions you think will affect the shot and a realistic decision about the kind of shot you want to play will give your mind all the information it needs to help you select the best club for the job.

DO NOT feed your mind with fearful or negative information such as "don't go into the rough" or "don't hit it into the bunker, out of bounds or in the pond." Your only job is to decide what shot you think is the best play under the circumstances and then tell yourself to *hit that shot.*

If your mind doesn't agree with your decision, you will get an uncomfortable feeling that means you should reconsider. Do not ignore this message! Your mind is only trying to help you avoid making a mistake. Take a moment to look the situation over again and see if perhaps you have missed something important or ought to consider trying something else.

Selecting a Club

When you have decided on the shot you want to play, let your sensing mind select the best club for the job. It will be the first one that you think of after you have decided on the shot and have taken into account the playing conditions. Don't give yourself a brain cramp by trying to analyze why that particular club first came into your mind. Trust your mind power and just take it out of the bag! Unless the conditions or the competitive circumstances have significantly changed since your earlier assessment, *always* go with the first club that comes into your mind.

If the conditions or circumstances *have* changed, you should start your preshot routine over and decide on the new shot you now want to play (or perhaps are forced to play by new competitive circumstances). If the wind has picked up or died down or has significantly changed direction, you may feel you need to reassess your club selection. To have a chance of winning a crucial hole or maybe even a tournament, you may have to try a shot you previously rejected as too risky. Whenever you are uncomfortable due to changed circumstances or conditions, start over and let your mind help you pick the best club for the new shot you have decided to play.

Before you move on to the next step in your preshot routine, you must be totally committed to the shot on which you decided and comfortable with the club you have selected. If doubt bubbles into your mind, it is a message that something is not quite right and you need to take another look at the situation. When you "feel good" about your shot selection and the club in hand "feels right," your mind has agreed that you are ready to move on.

This simple step is important to imprint confidence in your mind that the selected shot and the club in hand are the right choices and there is no need to doubt your selection or think about them further. To bolster that confidence, recall the feeling and the look of a really solid shot you have previously hit with that club. If you can't think of a specific good shot, simply remind yourself that you have hit plenty of solid shots before with the club you have selected. When you do this with a "positive tone" and a "can do" attitude, you are ready to continue with your preshot routine. On the other hand, don't expect to pull off some kind of miracle shot by falsely reassuring yourself that you can do something with which you have had little success or really don't know how to do. False bravado is a sure prescription for disaster on the golf course.

Making Practice Swings

There are two reasons to make practice swings before you set up to make your shot. The first is to alert your muscles and get them ready to make a swing. The second is to reinforce the feelings of your body movements. Whenever you make practice swings, concentrate on feeling your body and the club moving smoothly and rhythmically.

Some players like to make swings that accentuate their body movement. They like to feel their body move aggressively and hear the clubhead swish through the hitting area. Other players prefer to make more gentle or abbreviated swings, calmly sensing their feelings of smoothness and rhythm.

Whatever your choice, practice swings cue your mind and body that you are getting ready to go into action. Whatever club you have selected, you ought always to let your mind and body sense its feel by swinging it a few times. When you have finished making your practice swings, put the whole process completely out of your mind.

Visualizing Your Shot

Visualizing is simply the conscious use of our imagination to create pictures or images in our mind. Because we have the ability to imagine, we can "construct and see" all kinds of images in our mind. We each have complete control over the images we want to see, so we can construct images of good golf shots if we want to. In a nutshell, that is all there is to visualizing. The ability to visualize what you want to do is one of the most powerful mental contributions you can make to producing a good golf shot.

The purpose of visualizing is to "show and tell" your sensing mind exactly what you want to happen when you hit the ball. Developing your ability to visualize what you want the shot to look like, where you want it to land and where you want it to go, will contribute greatly to how successfully it will turn out. If your mind doesn't know what you want it to do, it can't help you. A mind that is undirected and unsure about what you want to do will add confusion and doubt to your preshot preparations and will likely wreck the ensuing shot.

People visualize in different ways. Some can clearly conjure up pictures in their mind's eye. Others get their imagination going with verbal information they feed into their mind. Some can combine their visual with their verbal imaginations. My golf imagination seems to work best with visual and verbal cues. You'll need to experiment with your own approach until you find what works best for you. However, because it is so powerful, I strongly encourage you to work at it until your imagination is showing you the kind of mind pictures you want to see. I also caution you not to expect to hit shots that are "over your head" just because you can conjure them up in your mind's eye. Visualizing will definitely improve your shotmaking. However, it is not a miraculous panacea that will suddenly start making great shots out of those you really aren't too good at. It will not make "silk purse shots" out of "sow's ear ability."

Each person's ability to use their imagination is different, so don't be concerned if your mind pictures are not in 3D living color or exquisitely detailed with birds and trees and clouds. The important thing is to give yourself the best imagined pictures and descriptions you can of *WHAT* you want to see happen. As you work on your golf imagination, you will begin to "see" more detail in your visualized pictures and you will hit more of your targets.

A Visualizing Process

Visualizing your shot is simple and takes only a few seconds. I start from a little behind my ball and look toward the general area where I want it to land. Then I select a specific landing spot or small landing area rather than some vague large area. The closer I am to my target, the smaller is my choice of a landing spot.

Choose the landing spot with the help of your sensing mind. As you look over where you want the ball to land, let your eyes wander around and "get acquainted" with the area for a few seconds. In a moment or so, you will notice that your eyes tend to focus on a particular spot or small area. Knowing the kind of shot you want to play, your mind will pick out a landing spot it feels will accomplish the result you want.

You can prove this works with the following simple test. With a ball in your hand, stand a few yards from the edge of a practice green as though you were going to make a short chip shot. Pick out a target hole and tell yourself that is where you want the ball to end up. Let your eyes roam around in the area between you and the hole; they will tend to settle on a particular spot or small area. This is where your mind feels you need to land your ball to come closest to the hole.

When your landing spot has been chosen, visualize it in a mental picture and retain it in your mind's eye. Then looking just at the ball in your hand, lob it at your imagined landing spot. After a few tries from different distances and to different target holes, you will notice that the closer you can land the ball to the spot your mind has chosen, the closer it will come to the hole. Hopefully, this will convince you that your sensing mind should *always* be in charge of picking out your landing spot.

Whenever you are visualizing a shot, always start by picking out a landing spot. From it, draw your eyes back to your ball while retaining its picture in your mind's eye. Then look back toward your landing spot and imagine the ball flying along a path you want it to take on its way to the target. If it works for you, quietly talk to your mind about what you are visualizing and tell yourself *WHAT* you want the ball to do and *WHERE* you want it to land.

Remember that your sensing mind will accept everything that you tell it. However, it cannot distinguish between yes and no, good and bad, desired and undesired and so forth. So when you are thinking and talking to yourself about what you want to see happen, always keep everything in positive terms. Only tell your mind what you *want* it to do, never what you *don't* want it to do. For example, never tell yourself *not* to hit it into the bunker, the pond, OB or the bushes.

On the tee, with my driver in hand, my mental talk might be: "I want the ball to land in the fairway right of the big tree. I want it to fly low and fade a little." With a short pitch and run shot I might tell myself: "I want to land the ball three feet onto the green and curve to the right toward the hole."

After I have "seen and talked" my imagined shot picture into my mind, I retain the image of the landing spot. I draw my eyes back along the target line to the ball and pick out an aiming spot a couple of feet or so in front of it. I keep the picture of the target area in my mind's eye and keep my eyes on the aiming spot.

As I get into the so-called "scoring range", within 100 yards or so of the green, my visualized picture of the shot and my mind talk become more detailed. For example, with a delicate pitch or chip shot, I feel the solid contact in my practice swings; I see the ball fly a short distance and hit on my landing spot and then roll toward the hole, curving a little right until it comes to a stop near the cup or even in the hole! Remember, we can imagine whatever results we want to see. There are no penalties for wanting the best. I always try to "see" the best possible outcome. To play your best golf it is essential that you always visualize the *results* you want from every shot.

With this process I have given my sensing mind all the information it needs to help me make the shot I want. I have told it the direction I want the ball to go, where I want it to land and what I want it to look like as it heads toward my target. I have also established an aiming spot on the target line to help get my body and my clubface lined up.

This is the kind of information your mind needs to help you prepare your setup and to control your body to execute your swing. If you feed it with positively stated information and then let it alone to do its work, it will do its utmost to produce the results you want.

Setting Up Your Address Position

When you have visualized the kind of shot you want to make and have picked out your target and an aiming spot, you are ready to set your body up to the ball. After visualizing my shot, I step around the ball while looking at my aiming spot. I keep my eyes on the aiming spot as I step into a preliminary setup roughly parallel to my target line. As I settle in, I draw a short imaginary line from the aiming spot back through the ball. With a good left-hand grip, which I put on the club after my practice swings, I aim the clubface down the target line and set it lightly behind the ball. Some people prefer to rest their aimed club on the ground; others can hover it above the ball and still keep it aimed as they move into their setup. Experiment with both approaches and then stick with whatever works best for you.

I keep the clubface aimed and then let my sensing mind help move my body around until I feel I'm in a balanced posture. I move my feet, hips, shoulders and head around until I sense they are parallel to my target line. Lastly, I complete my right-hand grip and confirm that the clubface is still pointing at the target. Only after completing this entire aiming and setup process do I move the club. From start to finish it only takes a few seconds. The key for me is always to get my club aimed on the target line before completing my setup, body and eye alignment and my right-hand grip.

You may worry about losing "sight" of your aiming line or target area during this process. Do not be concerned. When you earlier drew the imaginary aiming line in your mind's eye, it sensed where the line and the target are when it "saw" them. It retains a "sense of the target line" and will help direct the movement of your body to get it correctly lined up. It also retains a sense of the selected target area, and later when you are ready to refresh your target image just before you swing, your eyes will track right back along the line to the target area. Trust it, it works!

When I am set up and my posture and aim feel right, I make a few waggles by moving the clubhead back and forth smoothly on the target line. This loosens my wrists and forearms and alerts the rest of my swing muscles to get ready. My sensing mind perks up and is alerted that I'm about to make a shot. It also gets a quick picture of a mini-swing along the target line.

I look again at my target and reset its image in my mind's eye. Then I set the club in its take-away position. Unless I have shifted my feet or my body off the target line or moved my left-hand grip around after I got everything aimed my clubface and I will be on target.

When I settle my club in its takeaway position and have taken a last look at the target, I generally have the comfortable feeling of being ready. If I feel vaguely uncomfortable, if doubts creep into my mind or if my concentration is a little disturbed, I try to step away and regroup my mind, then re-aim and reset myself. If my concentration is really shattered, I try to start my preshot routine over from the beginning. The mental state I strive for just prior to starting my swing is to feel calm with no thoughts of my preparations, hazards, conditions of play or the upcoming shot. I try to be aware only of my body, my surroundings and the target image.

At the end of a preshot routine, you will have done everything necessary to get your mind and body ready to make your best swing effort. Your thinking then begins to quiet. You begin to ignore your surroundings and mentally shut out distractions for the next few seconds. This is the point in your preshot routine where you begin to turn your body and your swing over to your sensing mind.

All you need to do in the next few seconds is to let yourself trust your mind to make your swing. This is the most important part of your preshot routine. This is payoff time. Now is when you will focus your mind for a few seconds so it can take charge of your body and instinctively make the natural swing you have practiced and are capable of making.

Preshot Variations and Swing Thoughts

You can vary the elements, the order and the time frame of your preshot routine as long as you consistently repeat whatever process you choose before every shot. For example, some players prefer to secure their left hand grip before they begin their visualizing process. Some players can accurately aim their clubface by just looking at the target. And some players can accurately align their body and eyes instinctively.

Whatever works best for you should make up how and what you do in your personal preshot routine. This isn't science. It is a combination of many physical and instinctive senses that, as a whole, feel right to you. Work on developing your own routine, then stick with it. Practice it until it becomes a virtually automatic process.

A swing thought can be helpful if it reminds your sensing mind to do some important physical function. A swing thought must always be stated positively. It is best made just before you start your swing, and then you should put it entirely out of your mind.

To be most effective you should have only one swing thought that keys a whole series of correct actions. Some of the thoughts I have used are, "smooth rhythm," "relaxed arms" and "swing through the ball." I never think about doing any specific mechanical techniques or moves, as that would invite my thinking mind to get involved in my swing. The late smooth-swinging pro Julius Boros once said, "The middle of your swing is no time to give yourself a lesson." I believe him and you should too!

7.

TRUSTING YOUR SWING

You have reached the point in your shotmaking preparations where your preshot routine is complete. If you have one, you have recited your swing thought for the day. Your club is resting behind the ball. You are ready to swing. It is time to trust your swing.

Trusting your swing is the most important thing you must learn to have the best chance of making your best shots. This is where the confidence you have built by practicing your grip, setup and swing feels pays off. This is where the mental programming of your preshot routine pays off. This is where the confidence that you can hit solid shots becomes ultimately important. This is where your sensing mind takes over from your thinking mind.

To produce the best results, all physical activities must be controlled in that part of your mind that directs your body's physical movements. By my simple definition, this is the sensing part of your mind. You must learn to use it effectively if you are ever to fully "trust your swing."

From start to finish, trusting your swing takes only a few seconds, but these are the most important few seconds of all. If you don't completely entrust your body to your mind now, you will undo everything you have prepared yourself to do. The resulting shot will almost certainly not turn out as you wanted.

As your eyes return to the ball after your last look at the target, let your mind clear. Clear away all thoughts of your preshot preparations. It is extremely important not to have any lingering preshot thoughts in your thinking mind at this point. If a preshot thought should occur, acknowledge it and then let it go. If it persists, you should step away and regroup. When your thoughts are cleared away, then ignore your body's physical feelings and whatever is going on in your surroundings.

A second or two before your swing starts, let your mind go completely blank. I try to achieve a state of mind where I have no thoughts and where I am only dimly aware of my body and my surroundings. This lets my sensing mind take charge of making my swing. For me it is the pathway to a "focused" sensing mind. If thoughts intrude or I become too aware of body feelings or my surroundings, I acknowledge whatever it is and then let it go.

When my mind is focused, I am aware only of the ball and the club and a small area on which the ball is sitting. I feel calm and relaxed. I don't notice much, if anything, about my surroundings. I don't strongly feel any part of my body. I am aware of my eyes looking at the ball. My mind feels "empty." The ball and club may appear a little fuzzy, and sometimes my mind may even feel slightly "dreamy."

I ignore the club and don't stare intently at the ball. I am simply aware of my view, including the ball, the club and the background. My eyes feel very relaxed. I try to sense the muscles of my face relax. This is an easily recognizable signal to me that my sensing mind is taking over. I try not to do anything to disturb this sense of "focus" for the next few seconds.

My sensing mind "knows" it's time to swing the club when it sees that my thinking mind has become quiet. It is absolutely essential that your thinking mind remain completely quiet for the next few seconds. As long as you can keep it quiet, your sensing mind will take charge without any conscious effort on your part. It will start your backswing and manage and control the rest of your swing all the way through ball contact to your finishing follow-through. All you have to do during these few seconds is completely tune out your thinking mind while your sensing mind stays focused and does all the work. Although the explanation may seem long, the whole process takes no more than three or four seconds until the ball is on its way.

As you can imagine, getting your mind focused won't happen without a little practice. However, you will be pleasantly surprised at how quickly you learn to keep your focus undisturbed. In the beginning you will have to fight off intrusions of your thinking mind. Even before the club begins to move away from the ball, it will try to get involved. If you let it get into the act, it will chatter away about things it is seeing, sensing, physically feeling and worrying about. If permitted to become active, it will instantly overwhelm the control that your sensing mind has assumed over your swing. All the carefully programmed messages of your preshot routine will turn to mental mush with conflicting senses and feelings flying around in your head. The result of this brain chaos is muscle tension and stress. The resulting shot will range from disastrous to much less than you intended.

When you make a shot with your thinking mind chattering away you are virtually guaranteed to be less than thrilled with the results. When you experience this, and you will in every round, you will know how it feels to have lost your concentration. If your thinking mind starts to take over, step away a moment and regroup. You may even need to start your routine over from the beginning. With practice you will get much better at dealing with unwanted thinking just before and during your swing.

As you practice staying focused for those few critical seconds, note whatever creeps in to disturb you. You will likely begin to see a pattern of one or more recurring intrusions that you can work on acknowledging and then letting go. For example, were you startled a little as the club began to move away from the ball? Did a feeling of anxiety pop into your head as your backswing began to transition into your downswing? Did you become aware of your attention momentarily focusing on your feet or knees, your weight shifting, your shoulders turning or any other physical movements? Did something in your surroundings grab a moment of your attention? Did something other than golf — such as family, work, or you name it — pop into your mind?

All of these and other distractions and intrusions can occur as you try to remain focused for the few seconds just before and during your swing. Don't despair. Just keep practicing on getting your thinking mind to stay silent for a few seconds. If you persist, I think you will agree that the improved shotmaking results will have been well worth the effort.

Your sensing mind is a shy creature. It will turn off whenever your loudmouth thinking mind muscles into the picture. It retires to the sidelines when your thinking mind starts to chatter away. It takes patience, practice and confidence to learn how to keep your thinking mind from intruding in the few seconds just before and during your swing.

As you work on improving your mental golfing ability, your focus during the critical few seconds may vary from total concentration to being overwhelmed by thoughts, feelings and senses. Whenever you make a good shot with a well-focused mind, savor it and firmly plant the experience in your memory. It will serve as proof that a sensing mind in charge of your swing produces the best results. When a shot has gone astray — when you've lost your focus due to some distraction from your thinking mind — recognize the fact and move on.

Be patient with yourself. It's not easy to exclude your thinking mind from something with which it wants to be involved. Work first on minimizing these intrusions and then strive to eliminate them altogether. However, no matter how good you get at maintaining your focus, there will be times when a squeak or squawk from your thinking mind forces its way into the picture. The reality of mental golf is that we are unlikely to retain a perfectly focused mind for every shot and every putt.

On some occasions, however, you may stay perfectly focused for a critical shot, a large part of a round, or most rarely, throughout an entire round. Whenever that happens, you will know the incredible feeling of being "in the zone." In my experience the "zone" is a mystical feeling of great clarity, persistent calm and a focused sense of purpose that may result from a perfect balance between my thinking mind and my sensing mind. Whatever it is, it produces my best performance but is the most elusive of all my golfing experiences. I have no idea how to "turn it on" at will, but it surely is enjoyable when it happens! When you have an "in the zone" experience, and you will as you improve your mental golfing ability, don't question it or try to control it. Just go with the flow and enjoy the results.

As you get better at maintaining your focus, you will increasingly experience one of the true joys of golf. Your swing will just seem to happen. You will hardly feel anything but your rhythmically moving body and a sense of the club swinging through the ball. You will not consciously feel any particular part of your swing; sometimes you will hardly even feel the ball contact. As your swing is finishing and your head rotates up with the follow-through, you will see the ball flying toward your target. At that moment you will instantly know that you have hit a really good shot!

Exercising Your Sensing Mind

To help you get the feel of getting your sensing mind focused for a few seconds, try the following exercise. Sit or stand comfortably and close your eyes. Be aware of your body and your breathing for a few moments. Then ignore your body sensations, feelings and external distractions. Focus your attention only on your breathing. If thoughts or senses won't seem to go away, acknowledge them and then try to let them go. If you can't seem to clear your mind so you can focus, it's probably not the best day for you to be playing golf.

In the final step, ignore your breathing and focus your attention entirely on the blank space in front of your eyes. Put aside distractions of your thinking mind and your body sensations. At this stage you may notice your eye and eyelid muscles fluttering or twitching a little. Acknowledge the movement; then let them relax for a few seconds while focusing your attention only on the blank space in front of your eyes. Try to remain aware only of the blank space for a few seconds while all your other thoughts, senses and physical feelings stay in the background.

Then with your eyes open, try for a few seconds to duplicate the feeling of relaxed calmness that you felt when your attention was focused on the blank space in front of your eyes. Try to be only dimly aware of your body and surroundings. Try to bar thoughts and awareness of physical sensations from your mind. Feel your brow and eye muscles relax. Just let yourself "be" for a few seconds with no thoughts or senses at all. This is the state of mind and calm relaxation that I try to achieve when I see the ball and clubhead. I focus my sensing mind and let my thinking mind go blank.

As you practice, you will find that the time your mind remains calm and free of thoughts will easily last for several seconds before distractions reappear. You only need a few seconds in this calmly relaxed state which is free of thinking, for the focus of your sensing mind to take over and make your swing.

8.

PRESHOT AND MIND PRACTICE

You should work on developing your preshot routine and your mind focus whenever you practice. Every time you work on your game, you should always include some time to develop these habits and skills.

Have you noticed how often you hit the ball very well on the range when you are practicing or warming up, but for some mysterious reason, the solid ball contact you were making doesn't seem to go with you to the course? What could possibly be so different between the practice range and the golf course? You are the same golfer with the same clubs. The range balls don't know they are any different from the ball you play on the course.

Have you noticed how often you seem to be able to sink those pesky three and four footers on the practice green? Then later, when faced with the same putts on the course, you aren't able to buy one. Same golfer, same putter and probably the same ball. What gives?

For many, if not most golfers, the big difference between practice and the course is purely and completely mental. When you are practicing, there is no penalty for a poor shot or putt. On the course, one or more extra strokes go on your card when you goof up a shot or a putt. When practicing, your mind is generally quite relaxed, while you may be more keyed up when you're on the course. When you practice, your confidence is neutral at worst; on the course it can be clouded by doubts and fears of making bad shots.

In a mistaken attempt to help themselves "play better," many golfers let their thinking minds take charge when things start to go wrong. The result is usually a continuation or even worsening of their disappointing play. You can help yourself play better by trusting your sensing mind to make your swing. A consistently repeated preshot routine and good focus will tend to take your practice performance to the course. It will go a long way toward eliminating the doubts and fears that arise when you are not sure how to prepare yourself or what to expect from each shot or putt.

If you expect your practice to help you play better on the course, you must practice your whole game on the range and the putting green. This includes your entire preshot routine, focusing your mind and trusting your swing or your putting stroke. You must work on them as hard as you do on your swing mechanics if you expect to develop a strong habit pattern that will automatically repeat with each shot and putt. A preshot routine and focused sensing mind are just as much part of a good game as are good mechanics. In fact, without them it's hard to know what kind of results you are going to get.

When you have hit several solid shots with a particular club on the range, then hit a few balls preceded by your entire preshot and focus routine. Start your preshot routine practice by putting the club down and approaching the ball as though it is going to be a "real" shot. Just as you do when practicing your swing mechanics, pick out a target to shoot for. After each "full routine" shot, take a moment to review the results before you start into the next full routine practice shot. If the results aren't to your liking, ignore the shot and try again. When you get one you like, stop and savor it for a moment. Do exactly the same thing when you practice your putting.

After each swing or stroke, pay particular attention to how well you stayed focused all the way through impact. If you sensed a distraction, note what it was and where it occurred. Work on ignoring the previous distractions in your next practice swing or stroke. If you work on this enough, you will begin to recognize places or times where intrusions seem to regularly flash into your mind. You can then work on ignoring those momentary distractions the same way you work on the mechanics of your swing and putting stroke.

When I have made a particularly good practice shot or putt, I take a moment to enjoy the experience. In my mind's eye, I replay the feel of the solid contact and the rhythmic swing or stroke, and I "see" the ball as it flew or rolled toward my target. I congratulate myself for making a good shot or putt and then file the image away in my memory as proof that I *can* hit good shots and putts.

9.

PRE-GAME WARMUP

Warming up before a round should be just that — warming up your body and mind to play a round of golf. It is not the time to start working on a new swing thought, trying some new swing move or the latest tip you just read in your favorite golf magazine. This is *NOT* the time to practice!

Your practice and play has built a certain "muscle memory" into your mind. If you start tinkering with your "natural" swing now, you are hopelessly going to confuse your sensing mind when it is time for it to take over your swing on the course. Remember, it will try to do whatever you tell it to do. If you tinker with your swing as you warm up, you will invariably introduce doubt and confusion. Your sensing mind will be unable to sort it out on the course and much less able to manage the swing or stroke it already "knows" how to make.

The best time to practice new swing mechanics and thoughts is in a purely practice session or after the round is over. Notice how many of the pros go back to the practice range after a competitive round to work on some part of their swing. Remember, before a round your objective is quite different from practicing your swing.

The only objective of your pregame warm-up is to prepare your body and your mind to play golf — not to practice golf. I warm up my body by doing some gentle stretching, body turning and arm movements. I warm up my mind as I warm up my body by closing my eyes and sensing my body moving smoothly and rhythmically as I stretch and turn and bend. I take some time to check my grip and the sense and feel of turning my body and swinging relaxed arms. This short session, before I start to hit balls, helps me feel the rhythm of my swing and reinforces important preshot and swing feels.

Warming Up Your Swing

When you are ready to swing a club, pick out one you hit well with which to start. For most people this is a lofted club like the wedge through seven or eight irons. Begin by making several half or three-quarter swings without a ball to let your body and mind get the feel of a club in your hands. Concentrate on getting the feeling of smooth, rhythmic body movement as you swing the club back and forth.

When I feel loose and am making rhythmic swings, I set up with good posture and swing at an imaginary ball by picking out a spot on the grass. I make several swings without a ball, each time trying to clip or brush a spot on the grass where I have focused my eyes. I make these swings as hard as I wish as long as I stay solidly balanced and smoothly rhythmic. I particularly try to feel my shoulders and arms staying relaxed throughout my practice swings. When I have clipped or brushed a spot on the grass several times with well-balanced, rhythmic swings, I feel I have imprinted the feeling of that day's swing in my sensing mind.

The first few balls I hit with each warm-up club are with easy half or three-quarter swings. I don't worry about distance or hitting any particular target at that point. I just get the feel of swinging rhythmically and making solid contact with the ball. Rather than thinking about hitting the ball, I tell myself just to swing through the ball. When I feel loose and am making solid contact with abbreviated swings, I make some full swings focusing only on swinging the club smoothly *through* the ball.

To complete my warm-up with each club, I pick out a target and hit a few balls   incorporating my complete preshot and focus routine. I savor and remember the good warm-up shots and forget the others. When I have hit a few solid "full routine" shots, I pick another club and go through the same process again.

Some golfers feel they need to warm up with every club in the bag. Some hit a few balls with every other club; still others warm up by hitting balls with only a few clubs. Whatever your preference, it's a good idea to hit a few shots with the club you will be using on the first tee. This will bolster your confidence for that all-important first shot of the day.

When you have hit enough full shots to feel loose and have hit several really solid shots, end your practice session with a few short pitches and chips to get a feel for the more delicate swing of your short game. As you leave the practice range at the end of your warm-up session, reflect on the smooth rhythm and look of the solid shots you made. Ignore and forget the shots that were not so great.

Your warm-up session should not take more than twenty or thirty minutes. If you stay too much longer, you will pass a point where your body and mind are getting ready to play. You will start trying to "improve" by focusing attention on hitting practice shots and critiquing your performance rather than just warming up your muscles, your rhythm and your golf mind. Golfers are a little like geese are said to be. We wake up in a new golfing world every day. Warm up whatever swing you have that day rather try to change or fix something just before you start to play.

Don't hit warm-up balls too fast. The objective is not to hit as many balls as you can. Take your time and pace yourself between each shot to develop a feeling of relaxation rather than rushing through a bucket of balls. The effects of too much warm-up and one that progresses too fast will often be the creation of doubts and fears that are hard to keep out of your mind when you later tee it up for real.

Putting Warmup

On most courses, the practice greens are mowed at about the same height as the greens on the course. The speed at which the ball rolls on one will usually be similar to the other. To get a feel for the speed of the greens, try the following exercise when you are warming up.

Pick out a spot on the practice green not necessarily a cup about 25 or 30 feet away and hit a few balls to that spot. Take in the feeling of stroking smoothly through the ball and making solid contact. Hit a few of these "putts to nowhere" until you are satisfied you are making solid ball contact. When you have hit the ball solidly and have put several balls into a small circle, move on to putting a few balls toward a cup.

Some prefer to start by hitting longer putts and end by hitting a few short putts. Others prefer just the opposite. With your longer putts, concentrate more on getting a feel for distance than worrying too much about the line. On your short putts, hit them solidly and try to make as many as you can. Don't stay too long or your warmup putts will start to become practice putts along with unneeded tension. When you feel you are putting the ball solidly and have made a few, walk away from the practice green and just relax.

As I leave the practice green, I am confident that my body is ready, my mind is ready, and my swing and putting stroke are ready for the course. I try to take a few minutes to relax and let my warm-up session fade out of my mind. Now it's time to start just "letting it happen!"

10.

YOUR MIND ON THE FIRST TEE

Stepping up to the first shot of the day can stir up butterflies in even the best players. This is perfectly normal. Everyone's "nervous level" goes up a little on the first tee. However, this is where your preshot routine and your ability to focus your mind will give you a decided advantage. It will set you apart from players who have not learned to manage their minds and who step up to their first shot of the day without good physical or mental preparation. All too often players don't seem to have a clue about how to get their body and mind programmed to make that all-important first shot of the day.

When it is my turn to tee it up, I already have the club in hand with which I have hit several good shots during my warmup. I know I can hit the ball solidly with that club, so to get started I just need to focus my mind in the present and begin my preshot routine.

As you move through your preshot routine you will build confidence that it is preparing your mind and your body to make the shot you want. As you visualize the shot you want to make, you will also know that your mind is getting programmed. Finally, you will know that when you get your mind focused and you just let your swing happen, your mind will do its utmost to deliver the shot you want. Now is the time to trust yourself and just hit it!

II.

WHEN THE PRESSURE IS ON

Pressure is entirely self-imposed. On the course, pressure situations, such as an important putt, a tough shot or a delicate chip, happen all the time. Of course, some shots have more riding on their success than others. But the reality is that a shot or a putt played in a pressure situation is physically no different from any other tough shot or putt you have played successfully before.

The key to managing a pressure situation is first to put your mind in the present. Then be sure to run through your entire preshot or preputt routine in the same time frame and in the same relaxed manner you do with every other shot. When you see a competitor or your partner (heaven forbid!) deviate from their "normal" routine, you can be pretty sure that the pressure" has taken control; the upcoming shot will not be one of their best.

In even the most pressure-packed situations, your preshot routine will give you a focused sense of purpose that you can use to deflect negative thoughts and feelings of doubt. When you have run through your routine and are settling into your address position, your mind will be much calmer and more focused than if you did not have a preshot process to help get yourself prepared. Then, as you do with all your other shots, turn your swing or your putting stroke over to your sensing mind and just let it happen!

In his book *A Good Walk Spoiled*, John Feinstein recounts the pressure felt by Davis Love III, playing in a Ryder Cup alternate shot match with Tom Kite. As he stepped up on the first tee and was announced to the crowd, "Love didn't hear the polite applause. Somehow he managed to get his ball on the tee. He took a deep breath and went through his preshot routine. Everyone grew quiet. Love forced his mind to go blank. He checked his target and let twenty-five years of instinct take over. The ball flew in a high arc down the right side of the fairway. Perfect. Shakily, Love picked up his tee and smiled . . . ."

If, at any point in your routine, you don't feel right or your thinking mind starts a chattering binge, STOP and get a new grasp on the situation. Take a few deep breaths and start your routine over again with a new resolve to focus your mind and make a good shot or putt. In a pressure situation, whenever your preshot routine is interrupted for any reason, always start over. Performing your preshot routine and focusing your sensing mind in a "pressure situation" just as you do with all your other shots is the acid test of how well you can manage and control your golfing mind.

12.

THE SHORT GAME AND YOUR MIND

The short game is loosely defined as those shots made in the so-called "scoring range." This is generally considered to be within a hundred yards or so of the green. It also includes the deeper grass that frequently surrounds a green and the greenside bunkers. In the scoring range the objective is to get the ball close to the hole so you can hole out in one putt.

Other than putting, you can make more difference in your score more quickly by improving your short game play than anything else. The shots most commonly played near or around the greens are the pitch, the chip and the sand shot. There are many variations of these shots, and the mechanics of each are a little different.

Whichever "scoring" shot you play, the preshot routine is also slightly different from the routine that you do for your full shots. The differences pertain to being more specific about the location and size of your landing area and in to visualizing the results of the shot you want to make. In general, your visualizing process should become more detailed the closer you get to the hole.

You, of course, need to practice all of these short game shots to get a feel for controlling the flight distance and the rolling distance with various swings. Each of the scoring shots requires the utmost in sensing mind involvement. In particular, you must *absolutely* trust your swing to get your best results. Any thinking about mechanics or other thinking-mind interference will nearly always spoil these shots, sometimes with disastrous results.

The Pitch Shot

Of the three "scoring range" shots, the pitch shot is the most similar to a full shot. A pitch shot is executed with more clubhead speed, generally flies a greater distance and always flies higher than a chip shot. The greater clubhead speed adds backspin to the ball. More backspin lets you land a pitch shot on the green nearer the hole than a chip shot, yet settle its speed quickly so it doesn't run too far. Relative to its length, a pitch shot is generally one that uses maximum air time and minimum ground roll. Pitch shots can be played from as little as a few yards from the green to well out in the fairway or from most of the rough. The longer air time and generally shorter roll of a pitch shot are accomplished by slightly opening the clubface and making a fairly steep up-and-down swing that hits *down* on the ball.

A variation of the standard pitch shot is the so-called pitch and run shot. This shot is frequently called for when you are outside your chipping range, when you need to work your ball under an obstruction, such as a tree limb, or when you need the ball to land well short of your target and roll a goodly distance after landing. A pitch and run shot will fly much lower than a standard pitch shot, although it may have considerable air time. Because the clubface is slightly closed at impact, the ball will also roll a fair distance after landing. A pitch and run shot hit with a punch swing can frequently get you out of trouble.

Visualizing a pitch and run shot may be the most difficult of all the shots you play. The difficulty is in gauging the distance of the run after the ball lands and thus "seeing" the landing spot you want to hit. If there were ever a shot that you need to trust your sensing mind to see and hit, it is the pitch and run shot. You also need to practice pitch and run shots of various lengths so your mind can learn the feel of setting your body up and making the stroke.

The Chip Shot

A chip shot is executed with a fairly firm-wristed stroke that is not unlike a putting stroke. The basic idea is to get the ball rolling on the putting surface as soon as possible after the ball lands. The principal characteristic of a chip shot is short air time and longer roll time. Clubs used for chip shots range from a five iron up to sand wedges or pitching wedges for shorter shots where a little height is needed to pop the ball over some greenside obstruction like a short stretch of deep rough or a greenside bunker.

Some golfers feel most comfortable chipping with just one club, such as a seven iron. By practicing with one club, you can get the feel and see the results of increasing the loft by playing the ball a little more forward and slightly opening the clubface. You can also learn to feel and see the results of de-lofting the club by slightly closing the clubface and playing it a little farther back in your stance. The downside of one-club chipping is that you limit your opportunities to those where your "chipping club" can reliably clear "the bad stuff" and not roll too far past the hole. Try both approaches when you are practicing. Many players settle on a couple of clubs that will handle most of their chipping needs. For example, I use a 59-degree utility wedge for loftier and shorter running shots and a seven iron for lower and longer running shots.

For a chip shot to be most effective, you need to learn the maximum distance you can reliably control this most useful and versatile of all the "scoring range" shots. You need to teach your mind the various swing lengths and energies needed to chip the ball various distances with one or more clubs. And you need to teach your mind how the more firm-wristed stroke of a chip shot feels when played from grass of varying depth and thickness. The important idea to work on when you practice chipping is controlling the distance of the ball flight. You must trust your sensing mind every time you plan and make a chip shot.

Greenside Sand Shots

Perhaps no other shot in golf can cause more fear than the one awaiting a golfer whose ball has found a greenside bunker. Visions of impending disaster are common; many players trudge into the bunker with their minds clouded in a pall of dread. It doesn't have to be that way. With practice, a greenside bunker shot will be no greater challenge than any of your other short game shots. In fact, as you improve, you may even find yourself aiming at a bunker when you have a difficult approach shot.

The first job with your ball in a bunker is to *get the ball out of the sand* on the first try. As you improve your bunker play, you will get more comfortable executing a variety of shots and focusing on getting the ball close enough to hole it with one putt.

Your preshot preparation for a bunker shot should include getting your feet well-grounded below the surface layer of loose sand. When you work your feet into the sand, you can also get some idea of how firm or fluffy the sand is. This will help your sensing mind gauge the impact point on the sand and the swing effort you will make. As you do with your other scoring shots, pick out a specific landing spot and "see" the ball roll to the hole as you visualize the results you want from the shot.

There are several ways to play bunker shots. Your choices generally depend on factors such as the lie of the ball, the sand consistency and whether the ball needs to fly farther and stop quickly or float out softly and roll a distance. The mechanical keys to good bunker play are a stance that is slightly open to the line of the shot, a target on the surface of the sand two or more inches *behind* the ball, an open clubface and a wristy, steeply upright swing. The rhythm of your swing in a bunker should be very smooth.

To improve your ability to make these important scoring shots, don't hesitate to ask for help from a teaching pro or someone whose short game you particularly admire. This kind of instruction can, with the exception of better putting, do more to improve your scoring than anything else you can do. You may discover that making these scoring shots well might be the most fun of all because of how much they can affect your game.

13.

PUTTING AND YOUR MIND

In every round, putting accounts for more strokes made with the same club than with any other club in our bag. Putts can account for a third to over half of the strokes on our scorecard. Unfortunately, a three-foot putt counts the same as a booming tee shot or a great approach shot. Good putting will lower our score more quickly than anything else we can do to improve our game. By involving our sensing mind in our putting, our results can definitely be improved.

A putting stroke uses our body's most precise and delicate muscle control. Putting uses the smaller muscles in our fingers, hands, arms and shoulders. These muscle groups, particularly in our fingers, are fast-acting and can easily become tense and twitchy (the dreaded "yips") if they get the wrong kind of mind messages. A well prepared and focused sensing mind can help us sink more putts.

Basic putting mechanics include gripping the club comfortably, getting solidly balanced over the ball, keeping the body, head and eyes as still as possible, keeping the arms and hands as relaxed as we can and moving the putter smoothly and rhythmically. For me, a sound mental approach to putting is grounded in having confidence in my assessment of what the ball is "likely" to do as it travels toward the hole and confidence that I can make a sound stroke that hits the ball solidly. When I am comfortable and confident and move my putter smoothly and rhythmically, my sensing mind has the maximum opportunity to hit my putts on the right line at the right speed.

Because a putting stroke is somewhat like a miniature swing made with the shoulders, arms and hands, we must do the same things we do to prepare for a full swing. We must run through a consistently performed preputt routine prior to stroking the putt, and we must turn our stroke over to our sensing mind for execution.

My preputt routine starts by getting focused on the present. I try to put aside thoughts of putts missed in the past and concentrate on trying to make the one that I have now. Then I take a look at the conditions on the green between my ball and the hole and imagine how they will affect the roll of the ball. I visualize the ball rolling on my imagined path toward the hole just as I do with my other "scoring" shots. After lining up and settling my body to address the ball, I let my sensing mind make my stroke.

To get the best results from your putter, your routine must become a habit that is repeated before every putt is stroked. You will need to work on this as hard as you work on the routine you use for all your other shots. As your preputt routine improves and you build confidence that you are preparing yourself well, it will pay off with fewer putts per round and a lower score.

Assessing Green Conditions

The main job on the green before you hit your putt is to objectively assess the terrain and grass conditions along the path the ball will "most likely" take on its way to the hole. With practice you will learn to trust your sensing mind to "assess" and to "see" the effects of green conditions much better than you can possibly think out and calculate how much slopes, breaks, grain effects and so forth will affect the travel of the ball.

As I am looking at a putt from various angles, I carry on a mental conversation to tell my sensing mind what I am seeing. I don't try to make any judgments about how *much* I think a ball will break or how *hard* I need to hit it to get the ball to the hole. For a moment, I just let myself observe a fairly wide area — a path a couple of feet wide — between the ball and the hole. As I go about looking over the upcoming putt, I quietly talk to my mind about what I am seeing in that terrain. For example, I might tell my mind that it seems downhill or uphill, that it seems to be sloping to the right or the left, that there seems to be a fall line near the hole that may affect the ball in the last few feet or inches, that the grain seems to be growing into, with, or across the path to the hole. The important thing is that I am letting my sensing mind "see" what the general path to the hole looks like.

When you assess the conditions between your ball and the hole, it is important that you not make judgments about how much you think a putt will break or how fast it will be going up, down or across a slope. Just observe the terrain conditions and feed the information into your sensing mind. In the next step, you will use that information to visualize the line of your putt and see your ball rolling toward and into the hole.

Visualizing Your Putt

When you have observed the conditions your ball will encounter as it rolls to the hole, keep your sensing mind tuned in. You have already fed it with terrain and other observed information, so now let it help you pick the line of your putt.

I get behind my ball and let my eyes travel back and forth between the hole and the ball. I make these scanning looks several times without controlling the direction that my eyes are traveling. I just let them roam around and move along whatever path they want to as my view travels back and forth between the hole and the ball.

After a few scans, I notice my eyes beginning to follow a particular path between the ball and the hole. For me this path is a couple of inches wide. This is the line to the hole seen by my sensing mind. From this simple input, it will show me a particular line that it "sees" and on which it thinks the ball must roll along to go in the hole. As it sees the slopes and breaks, it also will have gotten an idea of how fast the putt must roll to stay on the line it has seen. You won't be able to consciously feel what is happening in your sensing mind, but when you learn to trust what it is showing you, you will be amazed at how accurate it is!

When your sensing mind has shown you the line and gauged the speed to the hole, visualize an imaginary line on the grass leading to the hole. My imagination seems to work best when I keep the line just a couple of inches wide. Then see the ball rolling along it and into the hole. After you have visualized this, draw your eyes back to your ball and pick out a spot a few inches in front of your ball. This is an aiming spot toward which you will start your putt rolling. Again, trust your sensing mind to pick that spot for you.

Before you move into your final stance and settle into your address, make a few rhythmic practice strokes, moving the putter face toward your aiming spot. Continuing to look at the aiming spot, settle your putter behind the ball with the face pointing squarely through the ball toward your aiming spot. Keeping the putter face on the line, shuffle everything around a little until you are comfortable and balanced over the ball.

When you are settled over the ball and your putter is lined up, take another look or two at the hole. Slowly let your eyes track back to your ball and pass over your aiming spot as they approach the putter head. Don't think about your readings of the green or anything else. If you will trust yourself to just let it happen, this last look will reset the target, distance, slope, fall line and overall terrain images that you earlier fed into your sensing mind. Then with all thoughts of your preparations out of your mind, turn your stroke over to your sensing mind just as you do every other shot.

Making Your Stroke

People putt as differently as they swing at their full shots. Some golfers can stand virtually immobile for agonizingly long times over a putt before they stroke it. Others address the ball, take a last look, and before you know it, the putt is on its way. The longer I stand over a putt before stroking it, the more likely stroke-wrecking thinking and muscle tension will overwhelm my sensing mind. After my last look, my stroke is under way in a few seconds.

As your eyes move from the hole back to your ball and the putter, let your sensing mind take over the same way you do with the rest of your game. Let your eyes relax and perhaps even let the ball and putter image get a little fuzzy. Keep your thinking mind completely quiet. Your stroke will just seem to start, and the path of the putter face and the force applied to the ball will be managed and controlled entirely by your sensing mind. All you have to do is keep your thinking mind quiet, keep your body well-balanced, your hands and arms relaxed and your head and eyes still until *after* the ball has been struck. Then you can look at the results. The chances are, if the ball doesn't go in the hole, it won't miss by much.

14.

FINAL THOUGHTS

As your mental golfing skills develop, you will increasingly recognize just how much your mind affects the results of every swing or stroke you make. Unfortunately, you will also notice that no matter how well you do your preshot routine, focus your sensing mind and rhythmically swing the club, some shots just don't turn out too well.

No matter how soundly your swing may be working, and how well you are managing your mind, the potential for a poor shot is always present. These unfortunate mishaps are related to one's individual skill levels, the conditions encountered on the course, tiny differences in one's body and mind from stroke to stroke and day to day and, of course, the whims of the golf gods.

For novice and journeyman players, a whole smorgasbord of mishaps is constantly lurking. They can make topped, fat, sliced, hooked or shanked shots at virtually any time, without warning. For top players these mishaps are rare, but missed greens and fairways happen in every round. The important point is for us not to expect perfection even though we have become a much better mental golfer. There is always the chance that we get a bad bounce, that the wind takes the ball for an unexpected ride, or that the ball just insists on landing in some awful place. Unfortunately, that is just the way golf is, and we need to to roll with the punches as we play.

This brings us to two more mental skills that we need to work on all the time to get the best results from our game. They are patience and enjoyment.

We need to be patient throughout every round we play. One or more misplayed shots or bad breaks are not the end of a round. Just as fast as things can go amiss, they can quickly turn spectacularly in our favor. However, if we let a bad shot or bad break get to us, it can mess up the whole day! We can greatly improve the chances that things will turn in our favor somewhere in the round if we will cultivate and practice patience with every shot and every hole.

It can be extraordinarily difficult to remain patient when your round is going poorly. Surprisingly, for many golfers it can be equally difficult to remain patient and play just one shot at a time when they are having a particularly good round. They start dwelling on "when the other shoe is going to drop" rather than accepting and enjoying their success. I think the key to managing both of these situations is the patience to play each shot and each putt just one at a time. Learn to keep your mind focused on what's important — the shot at hand, played to the best of your ability.

The last mental skill may be the single most important reason that we play golf — ENJOYMENT! Try to get the most enjoyment you can from every round. After all, except for the pros whose fortunes rise and fall with every shot, most of us are playing the game to have some fun and a break from our "other life."

Almost no one else in the world will either be affected or care about how well or how poorly you happen to be playing golf on a particular day. Your round of golf is not a major world shaping event. However, because golf is important to you, you need to enjoy the good shots and the good scores and try not to dwell on the shots and scores that were not your best. Pat yourself on the back occasionally and let yourself enjoy every solid shot and every good putt you make. Forget the other stuff.

Heaven knows it's not easy when you think your score will go out of sight and your competitors are beating your brains out. But if you can keep from losing your cool and beating yourself up, not only will you be a little happier at the end of the day, but — day in and day out — you will also play better golf.

TO ORDER YOUR COPIES OF

THE SIMPLE MENTAL SECRETS OF GOLF

by Stan Luker

MAIL   a copy of the coupon below with your check or money order to:

Chubasco Press
P. O. Box 21B
Balboa Island, CA 92662-0621

Please send _____ copy(ies) of *The Simple Mental Secrets of Golf* by Stan Luker to the following address:

Name: _____

Address: _____

City_____State:_____Zip:_____

Phone number _____

Method of payment:	Soft cover $15.95
Check: ❏	Shipping, per book
Credit card: ❏VISA ❏MasterCard	4th Class 3.00
	(allow 3-4 weeks)
Card number: _____	Priority mail 4.00
Name on card:	Sales tax,
_____	8.25% (CA) _____
Exp. date: _____/_____	Total Enclosed _____